2nd Workshop on Language in Social Media 2012

Held at the 2012 Conference of the North American Chapter of the Association for Computational Linguistics: Human Language Technologies (NAACL-HLT 2012)

Montreal, Quebec, Canada
3-8 June 2012

ISBN: 978-1-62276-549-2

Printed from e-media with permission by:

Curran Associates, Inc.
57 Morehouse Lane
Red Hook, NY 12571

Some format issues inherent in the e-media version may also appear in this print version.

Printed by Curran Associates, Inc. (2013)

For permission requests, please contact the Association for Computational Linguistics at the address below.

Association for Computational Linguistics
209 N. Eighth Street
Stroudsburg, Pennsylvania 18360

Phone: 1-570-476-8006
Fax: 1-570-476-0860

acl@aclweb.org

Additional copies of this publication are available from:

Curran Associates, Inc.
57 Morehouse Lane
Red Hook, NY 12571 USA
Phone: 845-758-0400
Fax: 845-758-2634
Email: curran@proceedings.com
Web: www.proceedings.com

This page intentionally left blank.

Introduction

Over the last few years, there has been a growing public and enterprise interest in 'social media' and their role in modern society. At the heart of this interest is the ability for users to create and share content via a variety of platforms such as blogs, micro-blogs, collaborative wikis, multimedia sharing sites, social networking sites etc. The volume and variety of user-generated content (UGC) and the user participation network behind it are creating new opportunities for understanding web-based practices and building socially intelligent and personalized applications. The goals for our workshop are to focus on sharing research efforts and results in the area of understanding language usage on social media.

While there is a rich body of previous work in processing textual content, certain characteristics of UGC on social media introduce challenges in their analyses. A large portion of language found in UGC is in the Informal English domain — a blend of abbreviations, slang and context specific terms; lacking in sufficient context and regularities and delivered with an indifferent approach to grammar and spelling. Traditional content analysis techniques developed for a more formal genre like news, Wikipedia or scientific articles do not translate effectively to UGC. Consequently, well-understood problems such as information extraction, search or monetization on the Web are facing pertinent challenges owing to this new class of textual data.

Workshops and conferences such as the NIPS workshop on Machine Learning for Social Computing, the International Conference on Social Computing and Behavioral Modeling, the Workshop on Algorithms and Models for the Web Graph, the International Conference on Weblogs and Social Media, the Workshop on Search on Social Media, the Workshop on Social Data on the Web etc., have focused on a variety of problem areas in Social Computing. Results of these meetings have highlighted the challenges in processing social data and the insights that can be garnered to complement traditional techniques (e.g., polling methods).

The goal of the workshop we propose is to bring together researchers from all of these areas but, in contrast to the above conferences and workshops, with a focused goal on exploration of characteristics and challenges associated with language on this evolving digital platform. We believe that the proposed workshop can serve as a focused venue for the linguistics community around the topic of language in social media.

We received great submissions, and it was a hard task to select the papers to accept. After spending a lot of time with reviews and the papers themselves and discussing each paper individually this is our final list of accepted papers. It should be a very interesting program!

Sara, Meena and Michael.

Organizers:

Meena Nagarajan (IBM Almaden)
Sara Owsley Sood (Pomona College)
Michael Gamon (Microsoft Research)

Program Committee:

John Breslin (U of Galway)
Cindy Chung (UTexas)
Munmun De Choudhury (Arizona State University, Microsoft Research)
Cristian Danescu-Niculescu-Mizil (Cornell)
Susan Dumais (Microsoft Research)
Jennifer Foster (Dublin City University)
Daniel Gruhl (IBM)
Kevin Haas (Microsoft)
Emre Kiciman (Microsoft Research)
Nicolas Nicolov (Microsoft)
Daniel Ramage (Stanford)
Alan Ritter (University of Washington)
Christine Robson (IBM)
Hassan Sayyadi (University of Maryland)
Valerie Shalin (Wright State)
Amit Sheth (Wright State)
Ian Soboroff (NIST)
Scott Spangler (IBM)
Patrick Pantel (Microsoft Research)
Andrew Gordon (USC)
Georgia Koutrika (IBM)
Hyung-il Ahn (IBM)
Smaranda Muresan (Rutgers)
Atefeh Farzindar (NLP Technologies)

Invited Speaker:

Marti Hearst, UC Berkeley

Table of Contents

Conference Program

Thursday, June 7, 2012

9:00	Introductions
9:15-10:15	Analyzing Social Media Text using Digital Humanities Techniques. Keynote talk by Prof. Marti Hearst, School of Information, UC Berkeley
10:15-10:30	Break
10:30-11:00	*Analyzing Urdu Social Media for Sentiments using Transfer Learning with Controlled Translations* Smruthi Mukund and Rohini Srihari
11:00-11:30	*Detecting Distressed and Non-distressed Affect States in Short Forum Texts* Michael Thaul Lehrman, Cecilia Ovesdotter Alm and Ruben A. Proano
11:30-12:00	*Detecting Hate Speech on the World Wide Web* William Warner and Julia Hirschberg
12:00-1:00	Lunch
1:00-1:30	*A Demographic Analysis of Online Sentiment during Hurricane Irene* Benjamin Mandel, Aron Culotta, John Boulahanis, Danielle Stark, Bonnie Lewis and Jeremy Rodrigue
1:30-2:00	*Detecting Influencers in Written Online Conversations* Or Biran, Sara Rosenthal, Jacob Andreas, Kathleen McKeown and Owen Rambow
	Re-tweeting from a linguistic perspective Aobo Wang, Tao Chen and Min-Yen Kan
2:30-3:00	Break
3:00-3:30	*Robust kaomoji detection in Twitter* Steven Bedrick, Russell Beckley, Brian Roark and Richard Sproat
3:30-4:00	*Language Identification for Creating Language-Specific Twitter Collections* Shane Bergsma, Paul McNamee, Mossaab Bagdouri, Clayton Fink and Theresa Wilson

Thursday, June 7, 2012 (continued)

4:00-4:30 *Processing Informal, Romanized Pakistani Text Messages*
Ann Irvine, Jonathan Weese and Chris Callison-Burch

4:30 Wrap Up

Analyzing Urdu Social Media for Sentiments using Transfer Learning with Controlled Translations

Smruthi Mukund
CEDAR, Davis Hall, Suite 113
University at Buffalo, SUNY, Buffalo, NY
smukund@buffalo.edu

Rohini K Srihari
CEDAR, Davis Hall, Suite 113
University at Buffalo, SUNY, Buffalo, NY
rohini@cedar.buffalo.edu

Abstract

The main aim of this work is to perform sentiment analysis on Urdu blog data. We use the method of structural correspondence learning (SCL) to transfer sentiment analysis learning from Urdu newswire data to Urdu blog data. The pivots needed to transfer learning from newswire domain to blog domain is not trivial as Urdu blog data, unlike newswire data is written in Latin script and exhibits code-mixing and code-switching behavior. We consider two oracles to generate the pivots. 1. Transliteration oracle, to accommodate script variation and spelling variation and 2. Translation oracle, to accommodate code-switching and code-mixing behavior. In order to identify strong candidates for translation, we propose a novel part-of-speech tagging method that helps select words based on POS categories that strongly reflect code-mixing behavior. We validate our approach against a supervised learning method and show that the performance of our proposed approach is comparable.

1 Introduction

The ability to break language barriers and understand people's feelings and emotions towards societal issues can assist in bridging the gulf that exists today. Often emotions are captured in blogs or discussion forums where writers are common people empathizing with the situations they describe. As an example, the incident where a cricket team visiting Pakistan was attacked caused widespread anguish among the youth in that country who thought that they will no longer be able to host international tournaments. The angry emotion was towards the failure of the government to provide adequate protection for citizens and visitors. Discussion forums and blogs on cricket, mainly written by Pakistani cricket fans, around the time, verbalized this emotion. Clearly analyzing blog data helps to estimate emotion responses to domestic situations that are common to many societies.

Traditional approaches to sentiment analysis require access to annotated data. But facilitating such data is laborious, time consuming and most importantly fail to scale to new domains and capture peculiarities that blog data exhibits; 1. spelling variations and 2. code mixing and code switching. 3. script difference (Nastaliq vs Latin script). In this work, we present a new approach to polarity classification of code-mixed data that builds on a theory called structural correspondence learning (SCL) for domain adaptation. This approach uses labeled polarity data from the base language (in this case, Urdu newswire data - source) along with two simple oracles that provide one-one mapping between the source and the target data set (Urdu blog data).

Subsequent sections are organized as follows. Section 2 describes the issues seen in Urdu blog data followed by section 3 that explains the concept of structural correspondence learning. Section 4 details the code mixing and code switching behavior seen in blog data. Section 5 describes the statistical part of speech (POS) tagger developed for blog data required to identify mixing patterns followed by the sentiment analysis model in section 6. We conclude with section 7 and briefly outline analysis and future work in section 8.

2 Urdu Blog Data

Though non-topical text analysis like emotion detection and sentiment analysis, have been explored mostly in the English language, they have also gained some exposure in non-English languages like Urdu (Mukund and Srihari, 2010), Arabic (Mageed *et al.,* 2011) and Hindi (Joshi and Bhattacharya, 2012). Urdu newswire data is written using Nastaliq script and follows a relatively strict grammatical guideline. Many of the techniques proposed either depend heavily on NLP features or annotated data. But, data in blogs and discussion forums especially written in a language like Urdu cannot be analyzed by using modules developed for Nastaliq script for the following reasons; (1) the tone of the text in blogs and discussion forums is informal and hence differs in the grammatical structure (2) the text is written using Latin script (3) the text exhibits code mixing and code switching behavior (with English) (4) there exists spelling errors which occur mostly due to the lack of predefined standards to represent Urdu data in Latin script.

Urdish (Urdu blog data) is the term used for Urdu, which is (1) written either in Nastaliq or Latin script, and (2) contains several English words/phrases/sentences. In other words, Urdish is a name given to a language that has Urdu as the base language and English as the seasoning language. With the wide spread use of English keyboards these days, using Latin script to encode Urdu is very common. Data in Urdish is never in pure Urdu. English words and phrases are commonly used in the flow integrating tightly with the base language. Table 1 shows examples of different flavors in which Urdu appears in the internet.

Different Forms of Data	**Main Issues**	**Example Sentence**
1. Urdu written in Nastaliq	1. Lack of tools for basic operations such as segmentation and diacritic restoration 2. Lack of sufficient annotated data for POS and NE tagging 3. Lack of annotated data for more advanced NLP	فوجی جوانوں کو کئی لوگوں سے غصہ آگیا *[The soldiers were angry with a lot of people]*
2. Urdu written in ASCII (English)	1. Several variations in spellings that need to be normalized 2. No normalization standards 3. Preprocessing modules needed if tools for Urdu in Nastaliq are to be used 4. Developing a completely new NLP framework needs annotated data	*Wo Mulk Jisko Hum nay 1000000 logoon sey zayada Loogoon ki Qurbanian dey ker hasil kia usi mulk main yai kaisa waqt a gay hai ?* *[Look at what kind of time the land that had 1000000's of people sacrifice their lives is experiencing now]*
3. Urdish written in Nastaliq	1. No combined parser that deals with English and Urdu simultaneously 2. English is written in Urdu but with missing diacritics	ٹی وی سٹیشن میں فون پر فون آنے لگے *[the phones rang one after the other in the TV station]*
4. Urdish written in ASCII(English)	**1. No combined parser that deals with English and Urdu simultaneously** **2. Issue of spelling variations that need to be normalized**	**Afsoos key baat hai . kal tak jo batain Non Muslim bhi kartay hoay dartay thay abhi this man has brought it out in the open.** ***[It is sad to see that those words that even a non muslim would fear to utter till yesterday, this man had brought it out in the open]***

Table 1: Different forms of using Urdu language on the internet

Blog data follows the order shown in example 4 of table 1. Such a code-switching phenomenon is very common in multilingual societies that have significant exposure to English. Other languages exhibiting similar behaviors are Hinglish (Hindi and English), Arabic with English and Spanglish (Spanish with English).

3 Structural Correspondence Learning

For a problem where domain and data changes requires new training and learning, resorting to classical approaches that need annotated data becomes expensive. The need for domain adaptation arises in many NLP tasks – part of speech tagging, semantic role labeling, dependency parsing, and sentiment analysis and has gained high visibility in the recent years (Daume III and Marcu, 2006; Daume III *et al.,* 2007; Blitzer *et al.,* 2006, Prettenhofer and Stein *et al.,* 2010). There exists two main approaches; supervised and semi-supervised.

In the supervised domain adaptation approach along with labeled source data, there is also access to a small amount of labeled target data. Techniques proposed by Gildea (2001), Roark and Bacchiani (2003), Daume III (2007) are based on the supervised approach. Studies have shown that baseline approaches (based on source only, target only or union of data) for supervised domain adaption work reasonably well and beating this is surprisingly difficult (Daume III, 2007).

In contract, the semi supervised domain adaptation approach has access to labeled data only in the source domain (Blitzer *et al.,* 2006; Dredze *et al.,* 2007; Prettenhofer and Stein *et al.,* 2010). Since there is no access to labeled target data, achieving baseline performance exhibited in the supervised approach requires innovative thinking.

The method of structural correspondence learning (SCL) is related to the structural learning paradigm introduced by Ando and Zhang (2005). The basic idea of structural learning is to constrain the hypothesis space of a learning task by considering multiple different but related tasks on the same input space. SCL was first proposed by Blitzer *et al.,* (2006) for the semi supervised domain adaptation problem and works as follows (Shimizu and Nakagawa, 2007).

1. A set of pivot features are defined on unlabeled data from both the source domain and the target domain
2. These pivot features are used to learn a mapping from the original feature spaces of both domains to a shared, low-dimensional real–valued feature space. A high inner product in this new space indicates a high degree of correspondence along that feature dimension
3. Both the transformed and the original features in the source domain are used to train a learning model
4. The effectiveness of the classifier in the source domain transfers to the target domain based on the mapping learnt

This approach of SCL was applied in the field of cross language sentiment classification scenario by Prettenhofer and Stein (2010) where English was used as the source language and German, French and Japanese as target languages. Their approach induces correspondence among the words from both languages by means of a small number of pivot pairs that are words that process similar semantics in both the source and the target languages. The correlation between the pivots is modeled by a linear classifier and used as a language independent predictor for the two equivalent classes. This approach solves the classification problem directly, instead of resorting to a more general and potentially much harder problem such as machine translation.

The problem of sentiment classification in blog data can be considered as falling in the realm of domain adaptation. In this work, we approach this problem using SCL tailored to accommodate the challenges that code-mixed data exhibits. Similar to the work done by Prettenhofer and Stein (2010), we look at generating pivot pairs that capture code-mixing and code-switching behavior and language change.

4 Code Switching and Code Mixing

Code switching refers to the switch that exists from one language to another and typically involves the use of longer phrases or clauses of another language while conversing in a totally different base language. Code mixing, on the other hand, is a phenomenon of mixing words and other smaller units of one language into the structure of another language. This is mostly inter-sentential.

In a society that is bilingual such as that in Pakistan and India, the use of English in the native language suggests power, social prestige and the status. The younger crowd that is technologically well equipped tends to use the switching phenomenon in their language, be it spoken or written. Several blogs, discussion forums, chat rooms *etc.* hold information that is expressed is intensely code mixed. Urdu blog data exhibits mix of Urdu language with English.

There are several challenges associated with developing NLP systems for code-switched languages. Work done by Kumar (1986) and Sinha & Thakur, (2005) address issues and challenges associated with Hinglish (Hindi – English) data. Dussias (2003) and Celia (1997) give an overview of the behavior of code switching occurring in Spanish - Spanglish. This phenomenon can be seen in other languages like Kannada and English, German and English. Rasul (2006) analyzes the linguistic patterns occurring in Urdish (Urdu and English) language. He tries to quantize the extent to which code-mixing occurs in media data, in particular television. Most of his rules are based on what is proposed by Kachru (1978) for Hinglish and has a pure linguistic approach with manual intervention for both qualitative and quantitative analysis.

Several automated techniques proposed for Hinglish and Spanglish are in the context of machine translation and may not be relevant for a task like information retrieval since converting the data to one standardized form is not required. A more recent work was by Goyal *et al.*, (2003) where they developed a bilingual parser for Hindi and English by treating the code mixed language as a completely different variety. However, the credibility of the system depends on the availability of WordNet[1].

4.1 Understanding Mixing Patterns

Performing analysis on data that exhibit code-switching has been attempted by many across various languages. Since the Urdu language is very similar to Hindi, in this section we discuss the code-mixing behavior based on a whole battery of work done by researchers in the Hindi language.

Researchers have studied the behavior of the mixed patterns and generated rules and constraints on code-mixing. The study of code mixing with Hindi as the base language is attempted by Sinha and Thakur (2005) in the context of machine translation. They categorize the phenomenon into two types based on the extent to which mixing happens in text in the context of the main verb. Linguists such as Kachru (1996) and Poplack (1980) have tried to formalize the terminologies used in this kind of behavior. Kumar (1986) says that the motivation for assuming that the switching occurs based on certain set of rules and constraints are based on the fact that users who use this can effectively communicate with each other despite the mixed language. In his paper he proposes a set of rules and constraints for Hindi-English code switching. However, these rules and constraints have been countered by examples proposed in the literature (Agnihotri, 1998). This does not mean that researchers earlier had not considered all the possibilities. It only means that like any other language, the language of code-mixing is evolving over time but at a very fast pace.

One way to address this problem of code-mixing and code switching for our task of sentiment analysis in blog data is rely on predefined rules to identify mixed words. But this can get laborious and the rules may be insufficient to capture the latest behavior. Our approach is to use a statistical POS model to determine part of speech categories of words that typically undergo such switches.

[1] http://www.cfilt.iitb.ac.in/wordnet/webhwn/

5 Statistical Part of Speech Tagger

Example 5.1 showcases a typical sentence seen in blog data. Example 5.2 shows the issue with spelling variations sometimes that occur in the same sentence

Example 5.1: *Otherwise humara bhi wohi haal hoga jo is time Palestine, Iraq, Afghanistan wagera ka hai ~ Otherwise our state will also be like what is in Palestine, Iraq, Afghanistan etc. are experiencing at this time*

Example 5.2: *Shariyat ke aitebaar se bhi ghaur kia jaey tu aap ko ilm ho jaega* ***key joh*** *haraam khata hai uska dil kis tarhan ka hota hey ~ If you look at it from morals point of you too you will understand the heart of people who cheat*

A statistical POS tagger for blog data has to take into consideration spelling variations, mixing patterns and script change. The goal here is not to generate a perfect POS tagger for blog data (though the idea explained here can be extended for further improvisation) but to be able to identify POS categories that are candidates for switch and mix. The basic idea of our approach is as follows

1. Train Latin script POS tagger (LS tagger) on pure Urdu Latin script data (Example 2 in table 1 – using Urdu POS tag set, Muaz *et al.*, 2009)
2. Train English POS tagger on English data (based on English tag sets, Santorini, 1990)
3. Apply LS tagger and English tagger on Urdish data and note the confidence measures of the applied tags on each word
4. Use confidence measures, LS tags, phoneme codes (to accommodate spelling variations) as features to train a new learning model on Urdish data
5. Those words that get tagged with the English tagset are potential place holders for mixing patterns

Word	**Act**	**Eng**	**LS Urdu**	**Urd CM**	**Eng CM**
and	CC	**CC**	NN	0.29	0.99
most	RB	**RB**	VM	0.16	0.83
important	JJ	**JJ**	VAUX	0.08	0.97
thing	NN	**NN**	CC	0.06	0.91

Zardari	NNP	NNP	**NN**	0.69	0.18
ko	PSP	NNP	**PSP**	0.99	0.28
shoot	VB	NNP	**JJ**	0.54	0.29
ker	NN	NNP	**NN**	0.73	0.29
dena	VM	NNP	**VM**	0.83	0.29
chahiya	VAUX	NNP	**VAUX**	0.98	0.21
.	SYM	.	**SYM**	0.99	0.99

Table 2. POS tagger with confidence measures

The training data needed to develop LS tagger for Urdu is obtained from Hindi. IIIT POS annotated corpus for Hindi contains data in the SSF format (Shakti Standard Format) (Bharati, 2006). This format tries to capture the pronunciation information by assigning unique English characters to Hindi characters. Since this data is already in Latin script with each character capturing a unique pronunciation, changing this data to a form that replicates chat data using heuristic rules is trivial. However, this data is highly sanskritized and hence need to be changed by replacing Sanskrit words with equivalent Urdu words. This replacement is done by using online English to Urdu dictionaries (www.urduword.com and www.hamariweb.com). We have succeeded in replacing 20,000 pure Sanskrit words to Urdu by performing a manual lookup. The advantage with this method is that

1. The whole process of setting up annotation guidelines and standards is eliminated.
2. The replacement of pure Hindi words with Urdu words in most cases is one-one and the POS assignment is retained without disturbing the entire structure of the sentence.

Our training data now consists of Urdu words written in Latin script. We also generate phonemes for each word by running the phonetic model. A POS model is trained using CRF (Lafferty, 2001) learning method with current word, previous word and the phonemes as features. This model called the Latin Script (LS) POS model has an F-score of 83%.

English POS tagger is the Stanford tagger that has a tagging accuracy of about 98.7%[2] .

5.1 Approach

Urdish blog data consists of Urdu code-mixed with English. Running simple Latin script based Urdu POS tagger results in 81.2% accuracy when POS tags on the entire corpus is considered and 52.3% accuracy on only the English words. Running English tagger on the entire corpus improves the POS tagging accuracy of English words to 79.2% accuracy. However, the tagging accuracy on the entire corpus reduces considerably – 55.4%. This indicates that identifying the language of the words will definitely improve tagging.

Identifying the language of the words can be done simply by a lexicon lookup. Since English words are easily accessible and more enriched, English Wordnet[3] makes a good source to perform this lookup. Running Latin script POS tagger and English tagger on the language specific words resulted in 79.82% accuracy for the entire corpus and 59.2% accuracy for English words. Clearly there is no significant gain in the performance. This is on account of English equivalent Urdu representation of words (e.g. *key* ~ their, *more* ~ peacock, *bat* ~ speak).

Since identifying the language explicitly yields less benefit, we showcase a new approach that is based on the confidence measures of the taggers. We first run the English POS tagger on the entire corpus. This tagger is trained using a CRF model. Scores that indicate the confidence with which this tagger has applied tags to each word in the corpus is also estimated (table 2). Next, the Latin script tagger is applied on the entire corpus and the confidence scores for the selected tags are estimated. So, for each word, there exist two tags, one from the English tagger and the other from the Latin script Urdish tagger along with their confidence scores. This becomes our training corpus.

The CRF learning model trained on the above corpus using features shown in table 3 generates a cross validation accuracy is 90.34%. The accuracy on the test set is 88.2%, clearly indicating the advantages of the statistical approach.

Features used to train Urdish POS tagger
Urdish word
POS tag generated by LS tagger
POS tag generated by English tagger
Confidence measure by LS tagger
Confidence measure by English tagger
Double metaphone value
Previous and next tags for English and Urdu
Previous and next words
Confidence priorities

Table 3. Features used to train the final POS tagger for Urdish data

[2] http://nlp.stanford.edu/software/tagger.shtml

[3] http://wordnet.princeton.edu/

Table 4 illustrates the POS categories used as potential pattern switching place holders

POS Category	Example
noun within a noun phrase	uski **life** par itna control acha nahi hai ~ its not good to control his life this much
Interjection	Comon Reema **yaar**! ~ Hey Man Reema! lol! ~ lol
Adjective	Yeh story bahut hi **scary** or **ugly** tha ~ This story was really scary and ugly
Adverb	Babra Shareef ki koi bhi film lagti hai, hum **definitely** dekhtai ~ I would definitely watch any movie of Babra Shareef
Gerund (tagged as a verb by English POS tagger)	Yaha **shooting** mana hai ~ shooting is prohibited here
Verb	Iss movie main I **dozed** ~ I slept through the movie
Verb	Afridi.. **Cool** off!

Table 4. POS categories that exhibit pattern switch

6 Sentiment Polarity Detection

The main goal of this work is to perform sentiment analysis in Urdu blog data. However, this task is not trivial owing to all the peculiarities that blog data exhibits. The work done on Urdu sentiment analysis (Mukund and Srihari, 2010) provided annotated data for sentiments in newswire domain. . Newspaper data make a good corpus to analyze different kinds of emotions and emotional traits of the people. They reflect the collective sentiments and emotions of the people and in turn the society to which they cater. When specific frames are considered (such as semantic verb frames) in the context of the triggering entities – *opinion holders* (entities who express these emotions) and *opinion targets* (entities towards whom the emotion is directed) - performing sentiment analysis becomes more meaningful and newspapers make an excellent source to analyze such phenomena (*Mukund et al.,* 2011). We use SCL to transfer sentiment analysis learning from this newswire data to blog data. Inspired by the work done by (Prettenhofer and Stein, 2010), we rely on oracles to generate pivot pairs. A pivot pair $\{w_S, w_T\}$ where $w_S \in V_S$ (the source language – Urdu newswire data) and $w_T \in V_T$ (the target language – Urdish data) should satisfy two conditions 1. high support and 2. high confidence, making sure that the pairs are predictive of the task.

Prettenhofer and Stein (2010) used a simple translation oracle in their experiments. However there exist several challenges with Urdish data that inhibits the use of a simple translation oracle.

1. Script difference in the source and target languages. Source corpus (Urdu) is written in Nastaleeq and the target corpus (Urdish) is written in ASCII
2. Spelling variations in roman Urdu
3. Frequent use of English words to express strong emotions

We use two oracles to generate pivot pairs.

The first oracle accommodates the issue with spelling variations. Each Urdu word is converted to roman Urdu using IPA (1999) guidelines. Using the double metaphone algorithm[4] phoneme code for the Urdu word is determined. This is also applied to Urdish data at the target end. Words that have the same metaphone code across the source and target languages are considered pivot pairs.

The second oracle is a simple translation oracle between Urdu and English. Our first experiment (experiment 1) is using words that belong to the adjective part of speech category as candidates for pivots. We augment this set to include words that belong to other POS categories shown in table 4 that exhibit pattern mixing (experiment 2).

6.1 Implementation

The feature used to train the learning algorithm is limited to unigrams. For linear classification, we use libSVM (Chang and Lin, 2011). The computational bottleneck of this method is in the SVD decomposition of the dense parameter matrix W. We set the negative values of W to zero to get a sparse representation of the matrix. For SVD computation the Lanczos algorithm provided by SVDLIBC[5] is employed. Each feature matrix used in libSVM is scaled between -1 and 1 and the final matrix for SVD is standardized to zero mean and unit variance estimated on $D_S \cup D_u$ (source subset and target subset).

6.2 Results

The domain of the source data set is limited to cricket and movies in order to ensure domain over-

[4] http://en.wikipedia.org/wiki/Double_Metaphone
[5] http://tedlab.mit.edu/~dr/SVDLIBC

lap between newswire data that we have and blog data. In order to benchmark the proposed technique, our baseline technique is based on the conventional method of supervised learning approach on annotated data. Urdish data set used for polarity classification contains 705 sentences written in ASCII format (example 6.1). This corpus is manually annotated by one annotator (purely based on intuition and does not follow any predefined annotation guidelines) to get 440 negative sentences and 265 positive sentences. The annotated corpus is purely used for testing and in this work considered as unlabeled data. A suitable linear kernel based support vector machine is modeled on the annotated data and a five-fold cross validation on this set gives an F-Measure of 64.3%.

Example 6.1:
General zia-ul-haq ke zamane mai qabayli elaqe Russia ke khilaf jang ka merkaz thea aur general Pervez Musharraf ke zamane mai ye qabayli elaqe Pakistan ke khilaf jang ka markaz ban gye . ~ negative

Our first experiment is based on using the second oracle for translations on only adjectives (most obvious choice for emotion words). We use 438 pivot pairs. The average F-measure for the performance is at 55.78% which is still much below the baseline performance of 64.3% if we had access to annotated data. However, the results show the ability of this method.

Our second experiment expands the power of the second oracle to provide translations to other POS categories that exhibit pattern switching. This increased the number of pivot pairs to 640. Increase in pivots improved the precision. Also we see significant improvement in the recall. The newly added pivots brought more sentences under the radar of the transfer model. The average F-Measure increased to 59.71%.

The approach can be further enhanced by improving the oracle used to select pivot features. One way is add more pivot pairs based on the correlation in the topic space across language domains (future work).

7 Conclusion

In this work we show a way to perform sentiment analysis in blog data by using the method of structural correspondence learning. This method accommodates the various issues with blog data such as spelling variations, script difference, pattern switching.

Precision (P %)	Recall (R %)	F-Measure (F %)
Phonemes (Roman Urdu)		
37.97	58.82	46.15
Metaphones based synonym mapping (adjectives)		
50.9	51	50.89
56.6	56.4	55.62
58.9	60.64	59.75
Precision (P %)	Recall (R %)	F-Measure (F %)
Metaphones based synonym mapping (adjectives + other POS categories)		
54.2	**64.3**	58.82
58.4	**60.85**	59.6
59.4	**62.12**	60.73

Table 5. SCL based polarity classification for Urdish data

We rely on two oracles, one that takes care of spelling variations and the other that provides translations. The words that are selected to be translated by the second oracle are carefully chosen based on POS categories that exhibit emotions and pattern switching. We show that the performance of this approach is comparable to what is achieved by training a supervised learning model. In order to identify the POS categories that exhibit pattern switching, we developed a statistical POS tagger for Urdish blog data using a method that does not require annotated data in the target language. Through these two modules (sentiment analysis and POS tagger for Urdish data) we successfully show that the efforts in performing non-topical analysis in Urdu newswire data can easily be extended to work on Urdish data.

8 Future work

Analyzing the test data set for missing and false positives, here are some of the examples of where the model did not work

Example 7.1: *"**tring tring tring tring..** Phone to bar bar bajta hai. **Annoying.**" ~ tring tring tring tring tring.. the phone rings repeatedly. Annoying.*

***Example 7.2**: "**bookon** ko padna tho ab na mumkin hai. Yaha thak mere friends mujhe **blindee** pukarthey hai" ~ cannot read books any more. Infact, my friends call me blindee.*

Example 7.3: *"Ek Tamana Hai Ke Faqt Mujh Pe Mehrban Raho, Tum Kise Or Ko Dekho To Bura Lagta Hai" ~ I have this one wish that destiny be kind to me If you see someone else I feel bad*

Our method fails to tag sentences like in example 7.1 where English verbs are used by themselves. Our POS tagger fails to capture such stand-alone verbs as verbs but tags them as nouns. Hence, doesn't occur in the pivot set.

Our second issue is with Morpho syntactic switching, a behavior seen in example 7.2. Nadhkarni (1975) and Pandaripande (1983) have shown that when two or more languages come into contact, there is mutual feature transfer from one language to another. The languages influence each other considerably and constraints associated with free morphemes fail in most cases. The direction and frequency of influence depends on the social status associated with the languages used in mixing. The language that has a high social status tends to use the morphemes of the lower language.

Example 7.4*: Bookon – in books, Fileon – in files, Companiyaa – many companies*

Clearly we can see that English words due to their frequent contact with Urdu grammatical system tend to adopt the morphology associated with the base language and used mostly as native Urdu words. These are some issues, if addressed, will definitely improve the performance of the sentiment analysis model in Urdish data.

References

Abdul-Mageed, M., Diab, M., and Korayem, M. 2011. Subjectivity and Sentiment Analysis of Modern Standard Arabic. *In proceedings of the 49th Meeting of ACL. Portland, Oregon, USA, June 19-24*

Agnihotri, Rama Kant. 1998. Social Psychological Perspectives on Second Language Learning. *Sage Publications, New Delhi*

Bharati, Askhar, Rajeev Sangal and Dipti M Sharma. 2005. Shakti Analyser: SSF Representation

Blitzer, John, Ryan McDonald, and Fernando Pereira. 2006. Domain adaptation with structural correspondence learning. *In proceedings of the 2006 Conference on EMNLP*, pp. 120–128, Sydney, Australia

Chang, Chih-Chung, Chih-Jen Lin. 2011. LIBSVM: a library for support vector machines. *In the ACM Transactions on Intelligent Systems and Technology*, Vol 2, no 27, pp 1-27

Dredze, Mark., Blitzer, John., Talukdar, Partha Pratim., Ganchev, Kuzman., Graca, Joao., Pereira, Fernando. 2007. Frustratingly Hard Domain Adaptation for Parsing. *Shared Task of CoNLL.*

Dussias, P. E. 2003. Spanish-English code-mixing at the auxiliary phrase: Evidence from eye-movements. *Revista Internacional de Lingüística Iberoamerican*. Vol 2, pp. 7-34

Gildea, Daniel and Jurafsky, Dan. 2002. Automatic Labeling of Semantic Roles, *Computational Linguistics*, 28(3):245–288

Goyal, P, Manav R. Mital, A. Mukerjee, Achla M. Raina, D. Sharma, P. Shukla, and K Vikram. 2003. Saarthaka - A Bilingual Parser for Hindi, English and code-switching structures. *In proceedings of the 11th Conference of the ECAL*

Hal Daume III and Daniel Marcu. 2006. Domain adaptation for statistical classifiers. *Journal of Artificial Intelligence Research*, Vol 26, pp. 101–126

Hal Daume III. 2007. Frustratingly easy domain adaptation. *In proceedings of the 45th Meeting of ACL*, pp. 256–263

International Phonetic Association (IPA). 1999. Handbook of the International Phonetic Association: A guide to the use of the International Phonetic Alphabet. *Cambridge: Cambridge University Press.* ISBN 0-521-65236-7 (hb); ISBN 0-521-63751-1

Joshi, Adithya and Bhattacharyya, Pushpak. 2012. Cost and Benefit of Using WordNet Senses for Sentiment Analysis. *LREC*, Istanbul, Turkey

Kachru, Braj. 1978. Conjunct verbs; verbs or verb phrases?. *In proceedings of the XIIth International Congress of Linguistics*. pp. 366-70

Lafferty, John, Andrew McCallum, Pereira. F. 2001. Conditional random fields: Probabilistic models for segmenting and labeling sequence data. *In proceedings of the 18th International Conference on Machine Learning,* Morgan Kaufmann, San Francisco, CA . pp. 282–289

Muaz, Ahmed, Aasim Ali, and Sarmad Hussain. 2009. Analysis and Development of Urdu POS Tagged Corpus. *In proceedings of the 7th Workshop on ACL-IJCNLP*, Suntec, Singapore, pp. 24–31, 6-7 August.

Mukund, Smruthi, Rohini K. Srihari. 2010. *A Vector* Space Model for Subjectivity Classification in Urdu aided by Co-Training, *In proceedings of the 23rd COLING*, Beijing, China

Mukund, Smruthi, Debanjan Ghosh, Rohini K. Srihari, 2011. Using Sequence Kernels to Identify Opinion Entities in Urdu. *In Proceedings of CONLL*

Nadkarni, Mangesh. 1975. Bilingualism and Syntactic Change in Konkani Language, vol. 51, pp. 672 C 683.

Pandaripande, R. 1981. Syntax and Semantics of the Passive Construction in selected South Asian Languages. *PhD dissertation. University of Illinois, Illinois*

Prettenhofer, Peter and Benno Stein. 2010. Cross-Lingual Adaptation Using Structural Correspondence Learning. *In proceedings of ACL*

Rasul, Sarwat. 2006. Language Hybridization and Code Mixing in Pakistani Talk Shows. *Bahaudin Zakriya University Journal 2nd Issue.* pp. 29-41

Roark, Brian and Michiel Bacchiani. 2003. Supervised and unsupervised PCFG adaptation to novel domains. In *Proceedings of the 2003 Conference of NAACL, HLT - Volume 1* (NAACL '03)

Rie-K. Ando and Tong Zhang. 2005. A framework for learning predictive structures from multiple tasks and unlabeled data. *In Jornal of Machine Learning. Res.*, Vol 6, pp. 1817–1853

Santorini, Beatrice. 1990. Part-of-speech tagging guidelines for the Penn Treebank Project. *University of Pennsylvania, 3rd Revision, 2nd Printing.*

Shimizu, Nobuyuki and Nakagawa, Hiroshi. 2007. Structural Correspondence Learning for Dependency Parsing. *In proceedings of CoNLL Shared Task Session of EMNLP-CoNLL.*

Sinha, R.M.K. and Anil Thakur. 2005. Machine Translation of Bi-lingual Hindi-English (Hinglish) Text. *10th Machine Translation summit (MT Summit X)*

Zentella, Ana Celia. 1997. A bilingual manual on how to raise Spanish Children.

Detecting Distressed and Non-distressed Affect States in Short Forum Texts

Michael Thaul Lehrman **Cecilia Ovesdotter Alm** **Rubén A. Proaño**
Rochester Institute of Technology
michael.lehrman@alum.rit.edu coagla@rit.edu rpmeie@rit.edu

Abstract

Improving mental wellness with preventive measures can help people at risk of experiencing mental health conditions such as depression or post-traumatic stress disorder. We describe an encouraging study on how automatic analysis of short written texts based on relevant linguistic text features can be used to identify whether the authors of such texts are experiencing distress. Such a computational model can be useful in developing an early warning system able to analyze writing samples for signs of mental distress. This could serve as a red flag, signaling when someone might need a professional assessment by a clinician.

This paper reports on classification of *distressed* and *non-distressed* short, written excerpts from relevant web forums, using features automatically extracted from input text. Varying the value of *k* in *k*-fold cross-validation shows that both coarse-grained and fine-grained automatic classification of affect states are generally 20% more accurate in detecting affect state than randomly assigning a distress label to a text. The study also compares the importance of bundled linguistic super-factors with a 2^k factorial model. Analyzing the importance of different linguistic features for this task indicates main effects of affect word list matches, pronouns, and parts of speech in the predictive model. Excerpt length contributed to interaction effects.

1 Introduction

Many people today deal with depression, post-traumatic stress disorder, and other mental disorders involving anxiety or distress, both diagnosed and undiagnosed. The societal costs of treating mental health are staggering. Sultz and Young (2011) estimate that the total mental health care treatment costs in the United States amount to more than USD 100 billion per year. The health care system in the United States generally focuses on treating patients' illnesses rather than on preventing their occurrence, and mental health care is no exception. Mental health diagnosis typically takes place after patients already show behavioral and physical symptoms associated with mental distress. Moreover, there are 33,000 suicides every year in the United States and, according to Matykiewicz et al. (2009; referencing Kung et al. (2008)), "[i]n the United States, suicide ranks second as the leading cause of death among 25-34 year-olds and the third leading cause of death among 15-25 year-olds" (p. 179).

Diagnosing mental illnesses is difficult. For example, depression has a prevalence of 19.5%, according to Mitchell et al. (2009), and is mostly diagnosed and treated by general practitioners. However, it is diagnosed correctly in only 47.3% of cases.

Commonly, the initial assessment of mental distress does not rely on clinical tests or advanced technology, and the evaluation of a patient is typically performed through the use of standardized questionnaires. A patient's answers are then compiled and compared with disease classification guidelines, such as the International Classification of Diseases or the Diagnostic and Statistical Manual, to guide the patient's diagnosis. However, these diagnostic methods are not precise and have high rates of false positives and false negatives. For example, in the United States, half of those who received mental health treatment did not meet the diagnostic criteria for a mental disorder (Kessler et al., 2005). In addition, societal and financial barriers prevent many people from seeking medical attention. In fact, in the USA, between 1990 and 2003, two-thirds of those with mental disorders did not receive treatment (Kessler et al., 2005). Many societies around the world stigmatize and discriminate against people with mental disorders, contributing to the unwillingness of individuals to acknowledge the problem and seek help (Michels et al., 2006; Fabrega, 1991).

It would be helpful if, e.g., military clinicians could effectively and non-invasively analyze soldiers' writing samples, social media posts, or email correspondence to screen service members for trouble coping with combat-related stress, to complement self-reporting or patient surveys. Careful thought would be required for access to such information so that it helps and not hurts. It seems useful as additional information for doctors.

We report on an initial study in which we analyze a smaller balanced dataset and experiment with inference of affect states at two different levels of affective granularity. Our work is based on Natural Language Processing (NLP) using supervised machine learning. We also discuss 2^k factorial, a method commonly used in engineering statistics, which has been successfully applied to many domains within engineering and product design for feature selection. Our work contributes initial reference values for what can be achieved by applying four fundamental supervised classification methods and text-based features to the challenging task of automatically classifying mental affect states in short texts based on just a small dataset. We discuss performance both in terms of different experimental setups, which linguistic features matter, and how labels confuse with each other.

2 Relevant previous work

Computational linguistics approaches have been applied to a range of challenging problems with impact outside the language technology field, e.g., to predict pricing movements on the stock market (Schumaker, 2010) or opinions on political candidates in event prediction markets (Lerman et al., 2008). In psychology, psychiatry, and criminology, studies with natural language data have found differences in behaviors for mental health patients or inmates with various mental health disorders (e.g., Andreasen and Pfohl, 1976; Harvey, 1983; Ragin and Oltmanns, 1983; Fraser et al., 1986; Endres, 2004; Gawda, 2010).

Recently, computational linguists have increasingly tackled problems in health care. For example, Zhang and Patrick (2006) automatically classified meaningful content in clinical research articles. Jha and Elhadad (2010) predicted how far breast cancer patients had progressed in their disease, based on discourse available in postings on web forums. As another example, Roark et al. (2007) explored the use of structural aspects of the language of individuals with mild cognitive impairment in assisting with such diagnostics.

More specifically in mental health, Yu et al. (2009) classified five forms of "negative life events" in text (p. 202). Pestian et al. (2008) were able to use machine learning, taking advantage of text characteristics to classify suicide notes as written by either "simulators" or "completers" as accurately as mental health experts (p. 96). The authors also found that emotional content was useful for the expert clinicians, but not for the automatic inference methods. However, this might indicate that the study did not consider an appropriate feature set. In comparison, Alm (2009) explored a more comprehensive feature set for automatic affect prediction in text. Matykiewicz et al. (2009) discriminated between suicide notes and control texts using automatic clustering techniques, and discovered sub-clusters within suicide writings. In 2011, Pestian et al. (2012) organized a challenge to determine emotions and meaningful information in notes by suicide completers. These latter investigatory efforts, while valuable, involved computationally analyzing suicide notes of individuals with advanced rather than earlier stages of mental distress.

Our work links fundamental NLP classification methods with a standard engineering statistics method. Since the publication of "Building a Better Delivery System: A New Engineering/Health Care Partnership" by the Institute of Medicine (IOM) and the National Academy of Engineering (NAE) in 2005, there has been increased attention to the potential of engineering to broadly improve U.S. health care delivery. The IOM-NAE report identifies the use of optimization techniques to support decision making as one of the most promising engineering tools and technologies that could help the health care system deliver "safe, effective, timely, patient-centered, efficient, and equitable" care (Reid et al., 2005, p. 1).

3 Conceptual model

We conceptualize the task of determining affect state as a classification problem. Formally, let t denote a text that expresses an affect state. Let k be the number of affect state classes $C = \{c_1, c_2, c_3, \ldots, c_k\}$, where c_i denotes a specific class label. The goal is to decide a mapping function $f : t \rightarrow c_i$ to obtain an ordered labeled pair *(t, c_i)*. The mapping is based on $F_t = \{f_1, f_2, \ldots, f_n\}$, describing *n* feature values, automatically extracted from the text *t*.

The label hierarchy is shown below in Figure 1. The coarse-grained level represents a binary classification problem: *distressed* vs. *non-distressed.* At a more fine-grained level, we distinguish four classes (see section 4 below): *high distress*, *low distress*, *response*, and *happy*.

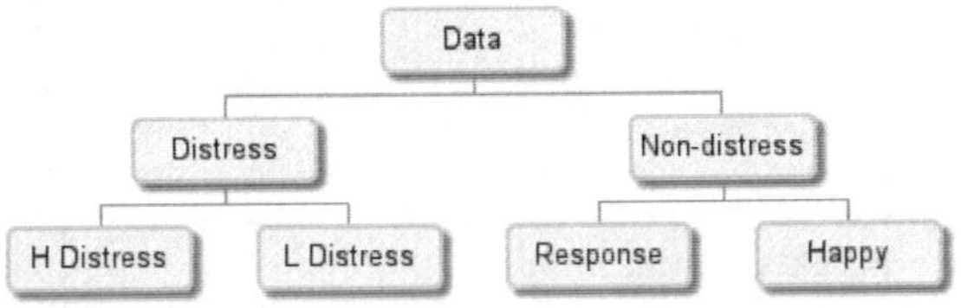

Figure 1. Class label hierarchy with two levels of granularity (binary vs. quaternary division of labels).

4 Dataset

There is currently no readily available text dataset for this problem. For this initial study, we prepared a small, annotated dataset of short written texts that represented relevant distinct, yet related, affect states. We manually collected a convenience (i.e., non-random) sample consisting of 200 posts from various public online forums dealing with mental well-being.[1] Forum posts were chosen because they are similar to other short digital social media texts, such as e-mails, online community posts, blog entries, or brief reflective writing that could be quickly gathered during a clinical session. We considered the text in the posts but not their titles.

4.1 Data annotation

Distressed and happy posts naturally divided into categories given the titles of the forums from which they were taken. Based on observation, we assumed that the distressed posts, all of which initiated new threads, were affectively distinct from *responses* to such threads, which had another polarity as they were meant to be reassuring and supportive. Therefore, we treated such responses as *non-distressed* posts. We recognize that a *response* represents a turn following an initial post. It is useful to explore how dialogic threading becomes part of affective language behaviors in social media (forums). The *happy* posts were included to represent the other extreme end of the affect spectrum.[2]

The dataset[3] was balanced such that 100 excerpts were *distressed*, 50 were *non-distressed responses*, and 50 were *non-distressed happy*. The *distressed* excerpts were then split further according to their distress intensity into *high* and *low* based on the annotator's perception, as seen in Figure 1. In an attempt to reduce personal bias, any post stating an active intent to harm someone or oneself was classified as *high distress*, while posts simply discussing bad feelings were usually classified as *low distress*. There were slightly more excerpts with low as opposed to high distress. Alm (2009) noted that expression of affect in language is often non-extreme. In a study of affective language in tales, Alm (2010) showed that affect is more often than not located in the gray zone between neutral and emotional. Table 1 shows the distribution of the excerpts according to four assigned class labels.

Class	**Raw count and % of total excerpts**	
High Distress	39	(19.5%)
Low Distress	61	(30.5%)
Response	50	(25.0%)
Happy	50	(25.0%)
Total	**200**	**(100%)**

Table 1. Distribution of excerpts by four classes.

Figure 2 provides affect class distribution by source. As expected, subforum topic seems related

[1] Excerpts were culled from forums that dealt with mental health states at BreastCancer.org and reddit.com. Manually inspecting data ensured that relevant texts were included, but we also acknowledge that data obtained by such a selection process might differ from data obtained by random selection.

[2] Short *happy* post example: "I now have my foot in the door of the custom cake decorating business. I start in customer service as a cashier/barista, work my way through frosting, and then either into wedding, birthday, or sculpted cakes! I have been unemployed for 3 months now and this is huge. It means I can start saving money again, paying my bills and loans, and all the while doing something I love!"

[3] Posts were self-annotated according to the title of the forum to which they were submitted (e.g., *r/depression* posts as *distress*, and *r/happy* posts as *happy* and *non-distress*). Self-annotation acknowledges that people experience subjective differences in their tolerance levels for distress. Only distressed posts were perceptually sorted into high or low distress based on data observations. Texts were also inspected to block invalid posts, spam, or irrelevant responses.

to the distribution of intensity of distressed posts (high vs. low).

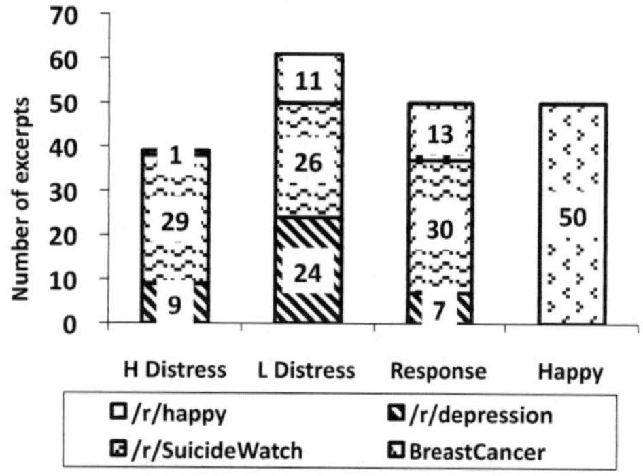

Figure 2. Excerpts by class and source.

5 Corpus linguistic analysis of dataset

Since this was an exploratory study, we conducted corpus linguistic analysis of the dataset by exploring descriptive statistics of linguistic and textual dimensions of the dataset.[4] As Table 2 shows, the collected corpus had 3,140 sentences, and totaled 49,850 words. There were on average 16 sentences or roughly 250 words in an excerpt.

Total excerpts	200
Total sentences	3,140
Total words	49,850
Average sentences per excerpt	15.70
Average words per excerpt	249.25
Average words per sentence	15.88

Table 2. Basic dataset statistics.

Table 3 shows basic statistics on text length.

Affect state and source	Sentences / excerpt	Words / excerpt
H Distress /r/SuicideWatch	19.8	300.0
H Distress /r/depression	31.1	399.7
L Distress breast cancer forum	16.5	297.5
L Distress /r/SuicideWatch	21.0	355.7
L Distress /r/depression	19.9	308.0
Response breast cancer forum	9.8	163.6
Response /r/SuicideWatch	14.3	218.2
Response /r/depression	13.4	219.9
Happy /r/happy	8.5	144.9

Table 3. Sentences and words per excerpt by affect state and source.

[4] We recognize that it would have been preferable to compute corpus statistics on a separate development dataset.

The statistics indicate that *happy* posts have the fewest sentences and words per excerpt, followed by the *responses*, ending with the *distressed* posts.[5]

In Table 4, we consider words per sentence as a metric independent of excerpt length, therefore avoiding potential selection bias. The average sentence length tended to be similar across forums.

Affect state and source	No. of excerpts	Words per sentence
H Distress /r/SuicideWatch	29	15.1
H Distress /r/depression	9	12.8
L Distress breast cancer forum	11	18.0
L Distress /r/SuicideWatch	26	16.9
L Distress /r/depression	24	15.5
Response breast cancer forum	13	16.6
Response /r/SuicideWatch	30	15.3
Response /r/depression	7	16.4
Happy /r/happy	50	17.1

Table 4. Length statistics by affect state and source.

We also examined exact lexical matches in polarity word lists,[6] with words having positive and negative connotation, which had been used before in Alm's work (2009). Positive words seemed favored in non-distressed posts (i.e., *responses* and *happy* posts). The opposite did not hold for *distressed* posts. Results are in Table 5.

We additionally examined the number of affect words present in each excerpt by considering four relevant affect word lists from Alm (2009), which were slightly expanded for this analysis (but less extensive than the polarity ones, yielding fewer matches overall).

Affect state and source	Positive	Negative
H Distress /r/SuicideWatch	18.0	20.0
H Distress /r/depression	24.0	24.0
L Distress breast cancer forum	21.0	15.0
L Distress /r/SuicideWatch	24.0	22.0
L Distress /r/depression	19.0	20.0
Response breast cancer forum	14.0	8.1
Response /r/SuicideWatch	17.0	13.0
Response /r/depression	17.0	13.0
Happy /r/happy	9.8	4.7

Table 5. Average polarity word list matches by affect state and source.

[5] Because only one BreastCancer.org post was classified as *high distress*, it was considered an outlier and thus excluded in presenting and discussing these tables.

[6] Positive and negative word lists contained 1915 and 2294 lexical items, respectively.

The average numbers of exact lexical matches from the word lists in all excerpts are shown in Table 6. For each affect word list (cf. columns), the highest and lowest values are in bold font. Table 6 shows that the number of average matches was low overall, and that in general, there were more matches with *sad* and *afraid* wordlists. However, *happy* posts showed slightly more overlap with the *happy* word list.

Affect state and source	Happy	Sad	Afraid	Angry
H Distress /r/SuicideWatch	0.9	1.8	2.1	**1.0**
H Distress /r/depression	1.1	**3.6**	3.3	**1.0**
L Distress breast cancer forum	**1.8**	1.6	1.9	0.5
L Distress /r/SuicideWatch	1.5	2.9	**4.0**	0.7
L Distress /r/depression	1.4	2.5	2.7	0.8
Response breast cancer forum	1.2	0.5	1.0	0.3
Response /r/SuicideWatch	1.3	2.0	2.4	0.5
Response /r/depression	**0.6**	1.1	1.3	**0.0**
Happy /r/happy	1.4	**0.4**	**0.5**	0.1

Table 6. Average emotion word list matches by affect state and source.

Lastly, because pronouns have been found important for linguistic analysis of mental health disorders or socio-cognitive processes (e.g., Andreasen and Pfohl, 1976; Pennebaker 2011), we explored this in the dataset based on the part of speech output from an NLTK-based tagger (Bird et al., 2009). Table 7 shows percentages of first-, second-, and third-person pronouns in the dataset.

Affect state and source	1st person	2nd person	3rd person
H Distress /r/SuicideWatch	77.1	0.9	22.0
H Distress /r/depression	56.1	12.0	31.9
L Distress breast cancer forum	63.0	10.9	26.1
L Distress /r/SuicideWatch	68.6	1.6	29.8
L Distress /r/depression	76.9	1.6	21.5
Response breast cancer forum	39.1	33.1	27.8
Response /r/SuicideWatch	23.1	46.1	30.8
Response /r/depression	21.3	56.9	21.8
Happy /r/happy	72.1	4.1	23.8

Table 7. % pronoun by person, affect state, and source.

There were few second-person pronouns in *distressed* and *happy* posts, but more in the responses, which had fewer first-person pronouns. This observation confirms that distressed and happy posts are *self-oriented*, but that responses, which reassure and reply to a thread initiator, are *other-oriented*. Perspective is thus another meaningful dimension of this affect dataset.

6 Computational modeling experiments

This initial study used three fundamental supervised classification methods: *Naïve Bayes*, *Maximum Entropy*, and *Decision Tree* (Bird et al., 2009). These allowed us to derive initial reference values which can be improved upon with more advanced techniques in future work. We also provide results for a fourth approach, Perkins' *Max Vote* method (2010), using the other three algorithms' predictions to give a joint prediction.

6.1 Feature set used for modeling

We developed a set of features based on the scholarly literature (e.g., Alm, 2009; Andreasen and Pfohl, 1976; Endres, 2004; Yu et al., 2009). The following features were automatically extracted from text, using Python, NLTK (Bird et al., 2009), and Perkins (2010): "bag of words" (BOW) with unique unigrams; excerpt length in sentences; excerpt and sentence lengths in words; positive vs. negative polarity word list matches; happy, sad, afraid, and angry affect word list matches; first-, second-, and third-person pronouns; and, finally, nouns, verbs, adjectives, adverbs, and pronouns.[7] Most features were initially examined both as a raw number and as a per sentence average. Features were discretized by considering how they deviated (more vs. less) from average values calculated from the corpus as a whole.[8] This resulted in 42 distinct feature types. Feature extraction was conducted the same way for train and test sets.

[7] Part of speech ratios were included due to an indication by Fraser et al. (1986) that verb patterns could be useful in discriminating manic patients from schizophrenics and the control group.

[8] The absence of a separate dataset for computing the averages allows a possibility of overfitting the data. However, we assume the averages are representative for similar texts and will be useful in future expanded model development.

6.2 Experiment 1: Classification at two levels

The computational experimental process is illustrated in Figure 3. In these experiments, the dataset is initially randomized and then evaluated with k-fold cross-validation, by repeating the classification process k times. Performance is thus reported as the average over k accuracy scores. The experiment explored five scenarios with $k = \{5, 10, 20, 100, 200\}$. The last scenario corresponds to a leave-one-out cross-validation (i.e., where the train set consists of *(N-1)* instances and the test set of one instance, and the procedure is repeated N times, where N is the total instances in the dataset).

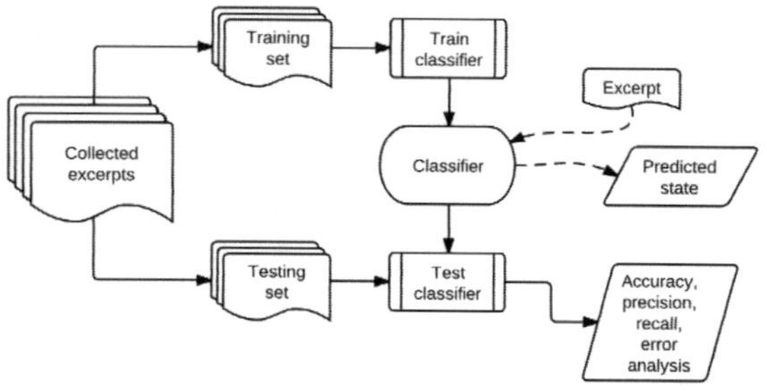

Figure 3. Computational experimentation process.

Figure 4 shows the accuracy for the coarse-grained binary classification problem which involved assigning either a *distressed* or a *non-distressed* label to a text excerpt. The majority class baseline for this is 50%, as half of the excerpts belonged to each of the two classes. Figure 4 shows that the classifiers average performance has a stable range with around 73-76% accuracy, across varying k-folds and across algorithms. This performance improves more than 20% over the majority class baseline, which is indicated by a line in Figure 4.

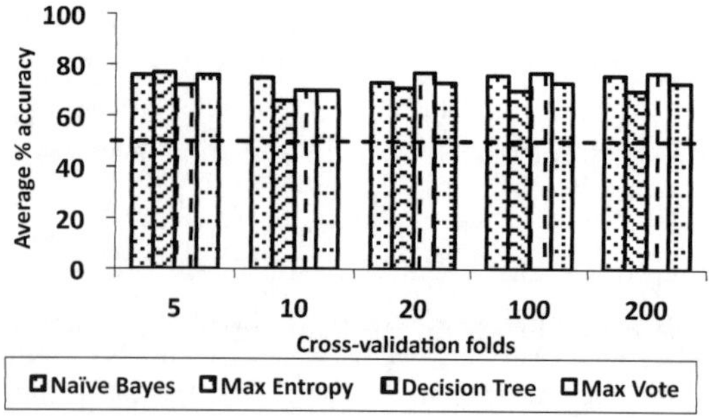

Figure 4. Classification accuracy for the coarse-grained classification scenario that considers two affect states: *distressed* and *non-distressed*.

Next, Figure 5 shows the results for classification at the fine-grained level which considers four affect classes: *high distress*, *low distress*, *response*, and *happy*. Here the majority class baseline is 30.5%. Four states yield around 54-57% accuracy. Again, that is more than a 20% improvement over the majority class baseline. The exception is Maximum Entropy, which performs poorly on this classification task.

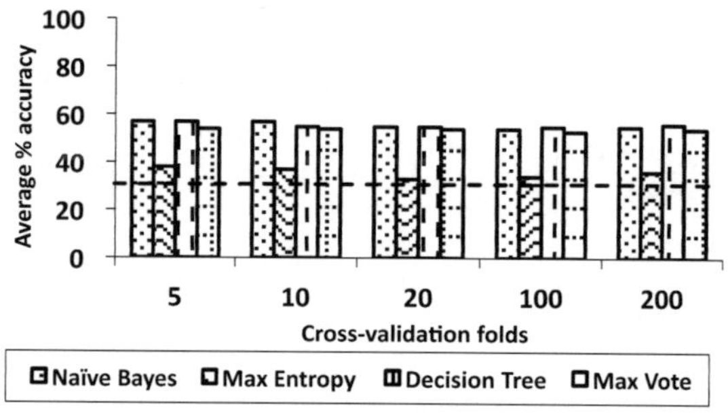

Figure 5. Classification accuracy for the fine-grained classification scenario that considers four states.

Inspecting the most relevant features from runs over the course of the study indicates that the number of second-person pronouns, which usually identified responses, and the number of verbs and fearful affect words per sentence are particularly important. In responding to a post, one uses more second-person pronouns in order to address the original poster. Again, this indicates that turn-taking impacts affective language behaviors.

A confusion matrix in Table 8 shows misclassification results for a select test fold of fine-grained classification. The shaded cells along the diagonal show how often the model correctly predicted an affect state. The other cells show where the model misclassified the affect state.

	Predicted			
Actual	H Distress	L Distress	Response	Happy
H Distress	**7.6%**	3.0%	1.5%	3.0%
L Distress	7.6%	**4.5%**	4.5%	9.1%
Response	.	.	**28.8%**	.
Happy	10.6%	3.0%	3.0%	**13.6%**

Table 8. A select confusion matrix.[9]

Looking at the *response* class, for example, the classifier correctly classified all of the actual

[9] This table shows results from a single test of a classifier. Due to the random test set, totals do not match the corpus totals.

response excerpts. This is likely due to the importance of second-person pronouns found in particular in the *response* excerpts. However, the classifier incorrectly labeled some excerpts in each of the other classes as *response*. Although this classifier was not as accurate for the other affect classes, the accurate option was the most commonly predicted class for both *high distress* and *happy*. This was not the case for *low distress*, however, which was more often predicted as *high distress* or *happy*. This can reflect the challenge of affect analysis in the gray zone between affect and neutrality, as lower emotional intensity decreases perceptual clarity. This finding is consistent with the previous literature, discussed above. A way to deal with this issue is to combine text analysis with other data analysis.

6.3 Experiment 2: Ablation study

An ablation study was performed to assess the accuracy with different features given the four fine-grained classes, using a $k = 5$ cross-validation. We ignore bag of words, which can result in many sparse features, to examine other types.

In Table 9, the first ablation step represents only length variables; the second adds polarity variables; the third adds affect variables; the fourth adds pronoun variables; and the fifth adds part of speech variables (in each case, to the features added in previous steps). Each test was done on all four supervised classification algorithms.

The results with this split of train and test data show that each addition to the feature set improved the accuracy of the model's predictions, except the part-of-speech features. This could be due to the particular data split, the order of the ablation steps, or the ablation feature groupings. Additionally, excluding BOW features did not have a clear negative effect on performance. Considering only length averaged 25.1% accuracy across classifiers; adding five feature types resulted in 54.5%.

	Classifier type				
	NB	**ME**	**DT**	**MV**	**Mean**
Length	.260	.225	.255	.265	.251
+ polarity	.295	.295	.390	.320	.325
+ affect	.430	.395	.365	.415	.401
+ pronouns	.590	.530	.485	.580	.546
+ POS	.595	.505	.505	.575	.545

Table 9. Ablation study results: four affect states fine-grained classification scenario (NB=Naïve Bayes, ME=Max Entropy, DT=Decision Tree, MV=MaxVote).

7 Engineering statistics applied to NLP

Choosing the right feature set remains a difficult, poorly understood process. Here, we report on a separate analysis using a 2^k factorial design, which is a common method from engineering statistics that can be used to quantitatively and systematically determine the effect and interactions that different linguistic feature types have on the assessment of the affect state of a text.[10] The outcome of this factorial design is a response formula that can be used to classify excerpts.

A 2^k experimental design assumes that a decision maker wants to determine how to express the effect of k different factors and their interactions on a response of interest. Given that the factors can take any possible value, the number of necessary experiments to statistically deduce such an expression can be quite large and expensive. Instead, a 2^k design limits each factor to only two levels (a high and a low value). The minimum number of experiments needed to deduce a model that explains the direct and interaction effects of k factors is 2^k. For example, a problem in which 5 factors are assumed to affect the value of a response requires executing 2^5=32 experiments, each with a unique arrangement of factor levels. Replications of these experiments are recommended to increase accuracy in the estimation of the term coefficients.

Having 42 candidate linguistic features that could influence an evaluator's decisions to categorize the distress state of a text would have required at least 2^{42} (over 4 trillion!) tests with different configurations of features. Therefore, we grouped related linguistic and textual features into five *super-factors*. For example, sentences per excerpt, words per excerpt, and words per sentence were all combined into a *length factor*. The super-factors chosen were: y_1 = length, y_2 = polarity, y_3 = affect, y_4 = pronoun, and y_5 = parts of speech.[11] Using five super-factors resulted in 32 (2^5) possible experimental combinations.

We assessed the 200 text excerpts based on all 42 linguistic features to get a numerical value for

[10] We adapt the regular terminology used in engineering statistics for discussing this approach. This means that k is used in a different sense in this section compared to above.

[11] BOW features were excluded here as well. The ablation study in section 6.3 also justifies their exclusion.

each super-factor. We then labeled each of these numerical values as *high* or *low*, based on the median of all 200 values for each factor and for each text. The super-factor label combinations for each of the 200 excerpts were then mapped to these 32 possible combinations. This mapping was used to generate a response formula (similar to a multi-attribute regression expression) that found the direct effect of the super-factors and their interactions on the distress evaluation.

We found that three main effects of the super-factors and four of their interactions were statistically significant. The significant super-factors were *affect*, *pronoun*, and *part of speech*. Although the main effect of *length* was not significant, its interactions with the *affect* and *pronoun* super-factors were significant.

The obtained expression for predicting the class of an excerpt is below. Each factor is a positive or negative 1, for high or low values, respectively:

$$\text{Response} = -0.377 + 0.2062y_3 + 0.355y_4 - 0.276y_5 + 0.1983y_1y_3 + 0.1928y_3y_4 - 0.197y_1y_3y_4 - 0.1704y_1y_3y_4y_5$$

Responses can range from –2 to 1, with –2 predicting *high distress*, –1 predicting *low distress*, 0 predicting *response*, and 1 predicting *happy*. This response formula could be tested as a prediction method on future data not used in its estimation.

We further propose using the 2^k factorial mechanism to systematically reduce the super-factors into simpler features. For example, because one of the super-factors did not show a significant main effect, we can assume that its linguistic features do not individually reflect distress or non-distress. Thus, one could reconfigure new super-features, assigning new values to the 200 excerpts, and repeat the analysis and remove any super-feature whose main and secondary effects are not significant. This iterative process should halt when we have new, redefined super-features that are significant in predicting the distressed and non-distressed states of the 200 excerpts. An analysis of residuals will serve as a control mechanism to reduce the number of iterations in the process.

8 Conclusion

If there were a way to automatically identify individuals with undiagnosed mental illnesses, it would be possible to recommend a clinical visit. The problem addressed by this paper was how to discriminate related affect states via computational linguistic analysis of short online writings.

We reported on an initial dataset from forums and corpus linguistic analysis, and found patterns in the data that merit further study. To predict distress states, we used supervised classification and explored super-features' importance with a 2^k factorial design, an engineering statistics method. We approach this problem from a linguistic perspective and pay extra attention to linguistic analysis and how distress is linguistically encoded. Not only do we report on effects by forum, distress state, emotion and polarity lexicon, etc., but our 2^k factorial analysis also rigorously clarifies which linguistic feature types contribute in statistically significant ways. Additionally, the ablation study conducted largely verified these findings.

Leave-one-out cross-validation is common with small datasets; we also show that varying *k* in the cross-validation does not impact results. There are benefits with smaller datasets and shorter texts. In clinical settings, data can be especially hard to obtain, and it is useful to understand the limitations and affordances of modeling with limited data. Similarly, it is important to understand how models perform on fundamental algorithms and shallow features extracted from text that can generalize to, for example, resource-poor languages.

While this data was adequate for exploratory investigation, a larger, clinical dataset would be less prone to selection bias. Combining text with other analysis information seems key in future work. Also, more advanced algorithms could yield more accurate predictions, as could iterations of the 2^k factorial analysis. Other aspects left for future study include the relationship between the individual affect states and their predictive linguistic features and experimentation with unbalanced data scenarios. Lastly, another area to pursue is using affect features for identifying linguistic patterns unique to online communication.

Acknowledgments

This work was supported by an RIT Seed Funding Award. We thank anonymous reviewers for comments. We also thank W. McCoy and R. Lehrman.

References

Cecilia Ovesdotter Alm. 2009. Characteristics of high agreement affect annotation in text. *Proceedings of the Fourth Linguistic Annotation Workshop, ACL 2010, Uppsala, Sweden, 15-16 July 2010*, 118-122.

Cecilia Ovesdotter Alm. 2009. *Affect in Text and Speech*. VDM Verlag, Saarbrücken.

Nancy J.C. Andreasen and Bruce Pfohl. 1976. Linguistic analysis of speech in affective disorders. *Archives of General Psychiatry*, 33:1361-1367.

Steven Bird, Ewan Klein, and Edward Loper. 2009. Natural Language Processing with Python. O'Reilly Media, Sebastopol, CA. *Natural Language Toolkit*, http://www.nltk.org/book.

Anna Dixon, David McDaid, Martin Knapp, and Claire Curran. 2006. Financing mental health services in low and middle income countries: equity and efficiency concerns. *Health Policy Plan*, 21:71-82.

Johann Endres. 2004. The language of the psychopath: characteristics of prisoners' performance in a sentence completion test. *Criminal Behaviour and Mental Health*, 14:214-226.

Horacio Fabrega, Jr. 1991. Psychiatric stigma in non-Western societies. *Comprehensive Psychiatry*, 32:534-551.

William I. Fraser, Kathleen M. King, Philip Thomas, and Robert E. Kendell. 1986. The diagnosis of schizophrenia by language analysis. *British Journal of Psychiatry*, 148:275-278.

Barbara Gawda. 2010. Syntax of emotional narratives of persons diagnosed with antisocial personality. *Journal of Psycholinguistic Research*, 39:273-283.

Philip D. Harvey. 1983. Speech competence in manic and schizophrenic psychoses: The association between clinically rated thought disorder and cohesion and reference performance. *Journal of Abnormal Psychology*, 92(3):368-377.

Mukund Jha and Noémie Elhadad. 2010. Cancer stage prediction based on patient online discourse. *Proceedings of the 2010 Workshop on Biomedical Natural Language Processing, ACL 2010, Uppsala, Sweden*, 64-71.

Ronald C. Kessler, Olga Demler, Richard G. Frank, et al. 2005. Prevalence and treatment of mental disorders, 1990 to 2003. *New England Journal of Medicine*, 352:2515-2523.

Hsiang-Ching Kung, Donna L. Hoyert, Jiaquan Xu, and Sherry L. Murphy. 2008. *Deaths: Final data for 2005. National Vital Statistics Report*, 56:1-121.

Kevin Lerman, Ari Gilder, Mark Dredze, and Fernando Pereira. 2008. Reading the markets: Forecasting public opinion of political candidates by news analysis. *Proceedings of the 22nd International Conference on Computational Linguistics (Coling 2008)*, 473-480.

Mark Lutz. 2009. *Learning Python* (4th Edition). O'Reilly Media, Sebastopol, CA.

Pawel Matykiewicz, Wlodzilaw Duch, and John P. Pestian. 2009. Clustering semantic spaces of spaces of suicide notes and newsgroup articles. *Proceedings of the Workshop on BioNLP, Boulder, Colorado*, 179-184.

Kathleen M. Michels, Karen J. Hofman, Gerald T. Keusch, Sharon H. Hrynhow. 2006. Stigma and global health: Looking forward. *Lancet*, 367:538-539.

Alex J. Mitchell, Amol Vaze, and Sanjay Rao. 2009. Clinical diagnosis of depression in primary care: A meta analysis. *Lancet*, 374:609-619.

Elias Mossialos, Anna Dixon, Josep Figueras, and Joe Kutzin. 2002. *Funding Health Care: Options for Europe*. Open University Press, Buckingham, UK.

James W. Pennebaker. 2011. *The Secret Life of Pronouns: What our Words Say about us.* Bloomsbury Press, New York.

Jacob Perkins. 2010. *Python Text Processing with NLTK 2.0 Cookbook*. Packt Publishing, Birmingham.

John P. Pestian, Pawel Matykiewicz, Michelle Linn-Gus, Brett South, Ozlem Uzner, Jan Wiebe, Kevin B. Cohen, and Christopher Brew. (2012). Sentiment analysis of suicide notes: A shared task. *Biomedical Informatics Insights*. 5 (Suppl. 1), 3-16.

John P. Pestian, Pawel Matykiewicz, and Jacqueline Grupp-Phelan. 2008. Using natural language processing to classify suicide notes. *BioNLP 2008: Current Trends in Biomedical Natural Language Processing, Columbus, Ohio*, 96-97.

Ann Barnett Ragin and Thomas F. Oltmanns. 1983. Predictability as an index of impaired verbal communication in schizophrenic and affective disorders. *British Journal of Psychiatry*, 143:578-583.

Proctor P. Reid, W. Dale Compton, Jerome H. Grossman, and Gary Fanjiang. 2005. *Building a Better Delivery System: A New Engineering/Health Care Partnership*. The National Academies Press.

Brian Roark, Margaret Mitchell, and Kristy Hollingshead. 2007. Syntactic complexity measures for detecting Mild Cognitive Impairment. *BioNLP 2007: Biological, translational, and clinical language processing, Prague*, 1-8.

Shekhar Saxena, Graham Thornicroft, Martin Knapp, and Harvey Whiteford. 2007. Resources for mental health: scarcity, inequity, and inefficiency. *Lancet*, 370:878-889.

Robert P. Schumaker. 2010. An analysis of verbs in financial news articles and their impact on stock price. *Proceedings of the NAACL HLT 2010 Workshop on Computational Linguistics in a World of Social Media, Los Angeles, California*, 3-4.

David M. Shepard, Michael C. Ferris, Gustavo H. Olivera, and T. Rockweel Mackie. 1999. Optimizing the delivery of radiation therapy to cancer patients. *SIAM Review*, 41(4):721-744.

Harry A. Sultz and Kristina M. Young. 2011. *Health care USA: Understanding its Organization and Delivery* (7th Edition). Jones and Barlett Learning, LLC, Sudbury.

C. Turrina, R. Caruso, R. Este, et al. 1994. Affective disorders among elderly general practice patients: a two-phase survey in Brescia, Italy. *British Journal of Psychiatry*, 165:533-537.

World Health Organization. 2005. *Mental Health Atlas*. WHO, Geneva, Switzerland.

Liang-Chih Yu, Chien-Lung Chan, Chung-Hsien Wu, and Chao-Cheng Lin. 2009. Mining association language patterns for negative life event classification. *Proceedings of the ACL-IJCNLP 2009 Conference Short Papers*, 201-204.

Yitao Zhang and Jon Patrick. 2006. Extracting patient clinical profiles from case reports. *Proceedings of the 2006 Australasian Language Technology Workshop*, 167-168.

Detecting Hate Speech on the World Wide Web

William Warner and Julia Hirschberg
Columbia University
Department of Computer Science
New York, NY 10027
whw2108@columbia.edu, julia@cs.columbia.edu

Abstract

We present an approach to detecting *hate speech* in online text, where hate speech is defined as abusive speech targeting specific group characteristics, such as ethnic origin, religion, gender, or sexual orientation. While hate speech against any group may exhibit some common characteristics, we have observed that hatred against each different group is typically characterized by the use of a small set of high frequency stereotypical words; however, such words may be used in either a positive or a negative sense, making our task similar to that of words sense disambiguation. In this paper we describe our definition of hate speech, the collection and annotation of our hate speech corpus, and a mechanism for detecting some commonly used methods of evading common "dirty word" filters. We describe pilot classification experiments in which we classify anti-semitic speech reaching an accuracy 94%, precision of 68% and recall at 60%, for an F1 measure of .6375.

1 Introduction

Hate speech is a particular form of offensive language that makes use of stereotypes to express an ideology of hate. Nockleby (Nockleby, 2000) defines hate speech as "any communication that disparages a person or a group on the basis of some characteristic such as race, color, ethnicity, gender, sexual orientation, nationality, religion, or other characteristic." In the United States, most hate speech is protected by the First Amendment of the U. S. Constitution, which, except for obscenity, "fighting words" and incitement, guarantees the right to free speech, and internet commentators exercise this right in online forums such as blogs, newsgroups, Twitter and Facebook. However, *terms of service* for such hosted services typically prohibit hate speech. Yahoo! Terms Of Service [1] prohibits posting "Content that is unlawful, harmful, threatening, abusive, harassing, tortuous, defamatory, vulgar, obscene, libelous, invasive of another's privacy, hateful, or racially, ethnically or otherwise objectionable." Facebook's terms [2] are similar, forbidding "content that: is hateful, threatening, or pornographic; incites violence." While user submissions are typically filtered for a fixed list of offensive words, no publicly available automatic classifier currently exists to identify hate speech itself.

In this paper we describe the small amount of existing literature relevant to our topic in Section 2. In Section 3 we motivate our working definition of hate speech. In Section 4 we describe the resources and corpora of hate and non-hate speech we have used in our experiments. In Section 5 we describe the annotation scheme we have developed and interlabeler reliability of the labeling process. In Section 6 we describe our approach to the classification problem and the features we used. We present preliminary results in Section 7, follow with an analysis of classification errors in 8 and conclude in Section 9 with an outline of further work.

---

[1] Yahoo TOS, paragraph 9a http://info.yahoo.com/legal/us/yahoo/utos/utos-173.html

[2] Facebook TOS, paragraph 3.7 https://www.facebook.com/legal/terms

2 Previous Literature

There is little previous literature on identifying hate speech.

In (A Razavi, Diana Inkpen, Sasha Uritsky, Stan Matwin, 2010), the authors look for Internet "flames" in newsgroup messages using a three-stage classifier. The language of flames is significantly different from hate speech, but their method could inform our work. Their primary contribution is a dictionary of 2700 hand-labeled words and phrases.

In (Xu and Zhu, 2010), the authors look for offensive language in YouTube comments and replaces all but the first letter of each word with asterisks. Again, while the language and the goal is different, the method may have some value for detecting hate speech. Their detection method parses the text and arranges it into a hierarchy of clauses, phrases and individual words. Both the annotation and the classification strategies found in this paper are based on the sentiment analysis work found in (Pang and Lee, 2008) and (Pang, Lee and Vaithyanathan, 2002).

3 Defining Hate Speech

There are numerous issues involved in defining what constitutes hate speech, which need to be resolved in order to annotate a corpus and develop a consistent language model. First, merely mentioning, or even praising, an organization associated with hate crimes does not by itself constitute hate speech. The name "Ku Klux Klan" by itself is not hateful, as it may appear in historical articles, legal documents, or other legitimate communication. Even an endorsement of the organization does not constitute a verbal attack on another group. While one may hypothesize that such endorsements are made by authors who would also be comfortable with hateful language, by themselves, we do not consider these statements to be hate speech.

For the same reason, an author's excessive pride in his own race or group doesn't constitute hate speech. While such boasting may seem offensive and likely to co-occur with hateful language, a disparagement of others is required to satisfy the definition.

For example, the following sentence does not constitute hate speech, even though it uses the word "Aryan".

> *And then Aryan pride will be true because humility will come easily to Aryans who will all by then have tasted death.*

On the other hand, we believe that unnecessary labeling of an individual as belonging to a group often should be categorized as hate speech. In the following example, hate is conveyed when the author unnecessarily modifies bankers and workers with "jew" and "white."

> *The next new item is a bumper sticker that reads: "Jew Bankers Get Bailouts, White Workers Get Jewed!" These are only 10 cents each and require a minimum of a $5.00 order*

Unnecessarily calling attention to the race or ethnicity of an individual appears to be a way for an author to invoke a well known, disparaging stereotype.

While disparaging terms and racial epithets when used with the intent to harm always constitute hateful language, there are some contexts in which such terms are acceptable. For example, such words might be acceptable in a discussion of the words themselves. For example:

> *Kike is a word often used when trying to offend a jew.*

Sometimes such words are used by a speaker who belongs to the targeted group, and these may be hard to classify without that knowledge. For example:

> *Shit still happenin and no one is hearin about it, but niggas livin it everyday.*

African American authors appear to use the "N" word with a particular variant spelling, replacing "er" with "a", to indicate group solidarity (Stephens-Davidowitz, 2011). Such uses must be distinguished from hate speech mentions. For our purposes, if the identity of the speaker cannot be ascertained, and if no orthographic or other contextual cues are present, such terms are categorized as hateful.

4 Resources and Corpora

We received data from Yahoo! and the American Jewish Congress (AJC) to conduct our research on hate speech. Yahoo! provided data from its news group posts that readers had found offensive. The AJC provided pointers to websites identified as offensive.

Through our partnership with the American Jewish Congress, we received a list of 452 URLs previously obtained from Josh Attenberg (Attenberg and Provost, 2010) which were originally collected to classify websites that advertisers might find unsuitable. After downloading and examining the text from these sites, we found a significant number that contained hate speech according to our working definition; in particular, a significant number were anti-semitic. We noted, however, that sites which which appeared to be anti-semitic rarely contained explicitly pejorative terms. Instead, they presented scientifically worded essays presenting extremely anti-semitic ideologies and conclusions. Some texts contained frequent references to a well known hate group, but did not themselves constitute examples of hate speech. There were also examples containing only defensive statements or declarations of pride, rather than attacks directed toward a specific group.

In addition to the data we collected from these URLs, Yahoo! provided us with several thousand comments from Yahoo! groups that had been flagged by readers as offensive, and subsequently purged by administrators. These comments are short, with an average of length of 31 words, and lacked the contextual setting in which they were originally found. Often, these purged comments contained one or more offensive words, but obscured with an intentional misspelling, presumably to evade a filter employed by the site. For common racial epithets, often a single character substitution was used, as in "nagger", or a homophone was employed, such as "joo." Often an expanded spelling was employed, in which each character was separated by a space or punctuation mark, so that "jew" would become "j@e@w@."

The two sources of data were quite different, but complementary.

The Yahoo! Comment data contained many examples of offensive language that was sometimes hateful and sometimes not, leading to our hypothesis that hate speech resembles a word sense disambiguation task, since, a single word may appear quite frequently in hate and non-speech texts. An example is the word "jew". In addition, it provided useful examples of techniques used to evade simple lexical filters (in case such exist for a particular forum). Such evasive behavior generally constitutes a positive indicator of offensive speech.

Web data captured from Attenberg's URLs tended to include longer texts, giving us more context, and contained additional lower frequency offensive terms. After examining this corpus, we decided to attempt our first classification experiments at the paragraph level, to make use of contextual features.

The data sets we received were considered offensive, but neither was labeled for hate speech per se. So we developed a labeling manual for annotating hate speech and asked annotators to label a corpus drawn from the web data set.

5 Corpus Collection and Annotation

We hypothesize that hate speech often employs well known stereotypes to disparage an individual or group. With that assumption, we may be further subdivide such speech by stereotype, and we can distinguish one form of hate speech from another by identifying the stereotype in the text. Each stereotype has a language all its own, with one-word epithets, phrases, concepts, metaphors and juxtapositions that convey hateful intent. Anti-hispanic speech might make reference to border crossing or legal identification. Anti-African American speech often references unemployment or single parent upbringing. And anti-semitic language often refers to money, banking and media.

Given this, we find that creating a language model for each stereotype is a necessary prerequisite for building a model for all hate speech. We decided to begin by building a classifier for anti-semitic speech, which is rich with references to well known stereotypes.

The use of stereotypes also means that some language may be regarded as hateful even though no single word in the passage is hateful by itself. Often there is a relationship between two or more sentences that show the hateful intent of the author.

Using the website data, we captured paragraphs that matched a general regular expression of words relating to Judaism and Israel [3]. This resulted in about 9,000 paragraphs. Of those, we rejected those that did not contain a complete sentence, contained more than two unicode characters in a row, were only one word long or longer than 64 words.

Next we identified seven categories to which labelers would assign each paragraph. Annotators could label a paragraph as anti-semitic, anti-black, anti-asian, anti-woman, anti-muslim, anti-immigrant or other-hate. These categories were designed for annotation along the anti-semitic/not anti-semitic axis, with the identification of other stereotypes capturing mutual information between anti-semitism and other hate speech. We were interested in the correlation of anti-semitism with other stereotypes. The categories we chose reflect the content we encountered in the paragraphs that matched the regular expression.

We created a simple interface to allow labelers to assign one or more of the seven labels to each paragraph. We instructed the labelers to lump together South Asia, Southeast Asia, China and the rest of Asia into the category of anti-asian. The anti-immigrant category was used to label xenophobic speech in Europe and the United States. Other-hate was most often used for anti-gay and anti-white speech, whose frequency did not warrant categories of their own.

5.1 Interlabeler Agreement and Labeling Quality

We examined interlabeler agreement only for the anti-semitic vs. other distinction. We had a set of 1000 paragraphs labeled by three different annotators. The Fleiss kappa interlabeler agreement for anti-semitic paragraphs vs. other was 0.63. We created two corpora from this same set of 1000 paragraphs. First, the *majority* corpus was generated from the three labeled sets by selecting the label with on which the majority agreed. Upon examining this corpus with the annotators, we found some cases in which annotators had agreed upon labels that seemed inconsistent with their other annotations – often they had missed instances of hate speech which they subsequently felt were clear cases. One of the authors checked and corrected these apparent "errors" in annotator labeling to create a *gold* corpus. Results for both the original majority class annotations and the "gold" annotations are presented in Section 7.

As a way of gauging the performance of human annotators, we compared two of the annotators' labels to the gold corpus by treating their labeled paragraphs as input to a two fold cross validation of the classifier constructed from the gold corpus. We computed a precision of 59% and recall of 68% for the two annotators. This sets an upper bound on the performance we should expect from a classifier.

6 Classification Approach

We used the template-based strategy presented in (Yarowsky, 1994) to generate features from the corpus. Each template was centered around a single word as shown in Table 1. Literal words in an ordered two word window on either side of a given word were used exactly as described in (Yarowsky, 1994). In addition, a part-of-speech tagging of each sentence provided the similar part-of-speech windows as features. Brown clusters as described in (Koo, Carreras and Collins, 2008) were also utilized in the same window. We also used the occurrence of words in a ten word window. Finally, we associated each word with the other labels that might have been applied to the paragraph, so that if a paragraph containing the word "god" were labeled "other-hate", a feature would be generated associating "god" with other-hate: "RES:other-hate W+0:god".

We adapted the hate-speech problem to the problem of word sense disambiguation. We say that words have a *stereotype sense*, in that they either anti-semitic or not, and we can learn the sense of all words in the corpus from the paragraph labels. We used a process similar to the one Yarowsky described when he constructed his decisions lists, but we expand the feature set. What is termed log-likelihood in (Yarowsky, 1994) we will call log-odds, and it is calculated in the following way. All templates were generated for every paragraph in the corpus, and a count of positive and negative occurrences for each template was maintained. The ab-

[3] `jewish|jew|zionist|holocaust|denier|rabbi|israel|semitic|semite`

solute value of the ratio of positive to negative occurrences yielded the log-odds. Because log-odds is based on a ratio, templates that do not occur at least once as both positive and negative are discarded. A feature is comprised of the template, its log-odds, and its sense. This process produced 4379 features.

Next, we fed these features to an SVM classifier. In this model, each feature is dimension in a feature vector. We treated the sense as a sign, 1 for anti-semitic and -1 otherwise, and the weight of each feature was the log-odds times the sense. The task of classification is sensitive to weights that are large relative to other weights in the feature space. To address this, we eliminated the features whose log-odds fell below a threshold of 1.5. The resulting values passed to the SVM ranged from -3.99 to -1.5 and from +1.5 to +3.2. To find the threshold, we generated 40 models over an evenly distributed range of thresholds and selected the value that optimized the model's f-measure using leave-1-out validation. We conducted this procedure for two sets of independent data and in both cases ended up with a log-odds threshold of 1.5. After the elimination process, we were left with 3537 features.

The most significant negative feature was the unigram literal "black,", with log-odds 3.99.

The most significant positive feature was the part-of-speech trigram "DT jewish NN", or a determiner followed by jewish followed by a noun. It was assigned a log-odds of 3.22.

In an attempt to avoid setting a threshold, we also experimented with binary features, assigning -1 to negative feature weights and +1 to positive feature weights, but this had little effect, and are not recorded in this paper. Similarly, adjusting the SVM soft margin parameter C had no effect.

We also created two additional feature sets. The *all unigram* set contains only templates that are comprised of a single word literal. This set contained 272 features, and the most significant remained "black." The most significant anti-semitic feature of this set was "television," with a log-odds of 2.28. In the corpus we developed, television figures prominently in conspiracy theories our labelers found anti-semitic.

The *positive unigram* set contained only unigram templates with a positive (indicating anti-semitism) log-odds. This set contained only 13 features, and the most significant remained "television."

7 Preliminary Results

7.1 Baseline Accuracy

We established a baseline by computing the accuracy of always assuming the majority (not anti-semitic) classification. If N is the number of samples and N_p is the number of positive (anti-semitic) samples, accuracy is given by $(N - N_p)/N$, which yielded a baseline accuracy of 0.910.

7.2 Classifiers

For each of the majority and gold corpora, we generated a model for each type of feature template strategy, resulting in six classifiers. We used SVM^{light} (Joachims, 1999) with a linear kernel function. We performed 10 fold cross validation for each classifier and recorded the results in Table 2. As expected, our results on the majority corpus were not as accurate as those on the gold corpus. Perhaps surprising is that unigram feature sets out performed the full set, with the smallest feature set, comprised of only positive unigrams, performing the best.

8 Error Analysis

Table 3 contains a summary of errors made by all the classifiers. For each classifier, the table reports the two kinds of errors a binary classifier can make: false negatives (which drive down recall), and false positives (which drive down precision).

The following paragraph is clearly anti-semitic, and all three annotators agreed. Since the classifier failed to detect the anti-semitism, we use look at this example of a false negative for hints to improve recall.

> *4. That the zionists and their american sympathizers, in and out of the american media and motion picture industry, who constantly use the figure of "six million" have failed to offer even a shred of evidence to prove their charge.*

Table 1: Example Feature Templates

unigram	"W+0:america"
template literal	"W-1:you W+0:know"
template literal	"W-1:go W+0:back W+1:to"
template part of speech	"POS-1:DT W+0:age POS+1:IN"
template Brown sub-path	"W+0:karma BRO+1:0x3fc00:0x9c00 BRO+2:0x3fc00:0x13000"
occurs in ± 10 word window	"WIN10:lost W+0:war"
other labels	"RES:anti-muslim W+0:jokes"

Table 2: Classification Performance

	Accuracy	Precision	Recall	F1
Majority All Unigram	0.94	0.00	0.00	0.00
Majority Positive Unigram	0.94	0.67	0.07	0.12
Majority Full Classifier	0.94	0.45	0.08	0.14
Gold All Unigram	0.94	0.71	0.51	0.59
Gold Positive Unigram	0.94	0.68	0.60	0.63
Gold Full Classifier	0.93	0.67	0.36	0.47
Human Annotators	0.96	0.59	0.68	0.63

Table 3: Error Report

	False Negative	False Positive
Majority All Unigram	6.0%	0.1%
Majority Positive Unigram	5.6%	0.2%
Majority Full Classifier	5.5%	0.6%
Gold All Unigram	4.4%	1.8%
Gold Positive Unigram	3.6%	2.5%
Gold Full Classifier	5.7%	1.6%

The linguistic features that clearly flag this paragraph as anti-semitic are the noun phrase containing *zionist ... sympathizers*, the gratuitous inclusion of *media and motion picture industry* and the skepticism indicated by quoting the phrase *"six million"*. It is possible that the first feature could have been detected by adding parts of speech and Brown Cluster paths to the 10 word occurrence window. A method for detecting redundancy might also be employed to detect the second feature. Recent work on emotional speech might be used to detect the third.

The following paragraph is more ambiguous. The annotator knew that GT stood for gentile, which left the impression of an intentional misspelling. With the word spelled out, the sentence might not be anti-semitic.

18) A jew and a GT mustn't be buried side by side.

Specialized knowledge of stereotypical language and the various ways that its authors mask it could make a classifier's performance superior to that of the average human reader.

The following sentence was labeled negative by annotators but the classifier predicted an anti-semitic label.

What do knowledgeable jews say?

This false positive is nothing more than a case of over fitting. Accumulating more data containing the word "jews" in the absence of anti-semitism would fix this problem.

9 Conclusions and Future Work

Using the feature templates described by Yarowsky we successfully modeled hate speech as a classification problem. In terms of f-measure, our best classifier equaled the performance of our volunteer annotators. However, bigram and trigram templates degraded the performance of the classifier. The learning phase of the classifier is sensitive to features that ought to cancel each other out. Further research on classification methods, parameter selection and optimal kernel functions for our data is necessary.

Our definition of the labeling problem could have been more clearly stated to our annotators. The anti-immigrant category in particular may have confused some.

The recall of the system is low. This suggests there are larger linguistic patterns that our shallow parses cannot detect. A deeper parse and an analysis of the resulting tree might reveal significant phrase patterns. Looking for patterns of emotional speech, as in (Lipscombe, Venditti and Hirschberg, 2003) could also improve our recall.

The order of the paragraphs in their original context could be used as input into a latent variable learning model. McDonald (McDonald et al, 2007) has reported some success mixing fine and course labeling in sentiment analysis.

Acknowledgments

The authors are grateful for the data and the support of Matthew Holtzman of the American Jewish Congress. We would also like to thank Belle Tseng, Kim Capps-Tanaka, Evgeniy Gabrilovich and Martin Zinkevich of Yahoo! for providing data as well as for their financial support. Without their support, this research would not have been possible.

References

[Choi et al 2005] Yejin Choi, Claire Cardie, Ellen Riloff, Siddharth Patwardhan, *Identifying Sources of Opinions with Conditional Random Fields and Extraction Patterns.* In *HLT '05* Association for Computational Linguistics Stroudsburg, PA, USA, pp. 355-362, 2005

[Yarowsky 1994] David Yarowsky, *Decision Lists for Lexical Ambiguity Resolution: Application to Accent Restoration in Spanish and French.* In *ACL-94*, Stroudsburg, PA, pp. 88-95, 1994

[Yarowsky 1995] David Yarowsky, *Unsupervised Word Sense Disambiguation Rivaling Supervised Methods.* In *ACL-95*, Cambridge, MA, pp. 189-196, 1995.

[Nockleby 2000] John T. Nockleby, *Hate Speech.* In *Encyclopedia of the American Constitution* (2nd ed., edited by Leonard W. Levy, Kenneth L. Karst et al., New York: Macmillan, 2000), pp. 1277-1279 (see `http://www.jiffynotes.com/a_study_guides/book_notes/eamc_03/eamc_03_01193.html`)

[Stephens-Davidowitz 2011] Seth Stephens-Davidowitz, *The Effects of Racial Animus on Voting: Evidence Using Google Search Data* `http://www.people.fas.harvard.edu/~sstephen/papers/RacialAnimusAndVotingSethStephensDavidowitz.pdf`

[McDonald et al 2007] McDonald, R. Hannan, K. Neylon, T. Wells, M. Reynar, J. *Structured Models for Fine-to-Coarse Sentiment Analysis.* In *ANNUAL MEETING- ASSOCIATION FOR COMPUTATIONAL LINGUISTICS* 2007, CONF 45; VOL 1, pages 432-439

[Pang and Lee 2008] Pang, Bo and Lee, Lillian, *Opinion Mining and Sentiment Analysis.* In *Foundations and Trends in Information Retrieval*, issue 1-2, vol. 2, Now Publishers Inc., Hanover, MA, USA, 2008 pp. 1–135

[Pang, Lee and Vaithyanathan 2002] Pang, Bo and Lee, Lillian and Vaithyanathan, Shivakumar *Thumbs up?: sentiment classification using machine learning techniques.* In *Proceedings of the ACL-02 conference on Empirical methods in natural language processing - Volume 10*, Association for Computational Linguistics, Stroudsburg, PA, USA, 2002 pp. 79-86

[Qiu et al 2009] Qiu, Guang and Liu, Bing and Bu, Jiajun and Chen, Chun *Expanding domain sentiment lexicon through double propagation.* In *Proceedings of the 21st international jont conference on Artificial intelligence*, Morgan Kaufmann Publishers Inc. San Francisco, CA, USA, 2009 pp. 1199-1204

[Joachims 1999] *Making large-Scale SVM Learning Practical. Advances in Kernel Methods - Support Vector Learning*, B. Schlkopf and C. Burges and A. Smola (ed.), MIT-Press, 1999.

[Koo, Carreras and Collins 2008] *Simple Semi-supervised Dependency Parsing* In *Proc. ACL/HLT* 2008

[Xu and Zhu 2010] *Filtering Offensive Language in Online Communities using Grammatical Relations*

[A Razavi, Diana Inkpen, Sasha Uritsky, Stan Matwin 2010] *Offensive Language Detection Using Multi-level Classification* In *Advances in Artificial Intelligence* Springer, 2010, pp. 1627

[Attenberg and Provost 2010] *Why Label When You Can Search?: Alternatives to active learning for applying human resources to build classification models under extreme class imbalance,* KDD 2010

[Lipscombe, Venditti and Hirschberg 2003] *Classifying Subject Ratings of Emotional Speech Using Acoustic Features.* In *Proceedings of Eurospeech* 2003, Geneva.

A Demographic Analysis of Online Sentiment during Hurricane Irene

Benjamin Mandel*, **Aron Culotta***, **John Boulahanis**+,
Danielle Stark+, **Bonnie Lewis**+, **Jeremy Rodrigue**+
*Department of Computer Science and Industrial Technology
+Department of Sociology and Criminal Justice
Southeastern Louisiana University
Hammond, LA 70402

Abstract

We examine the response to the recent natural disaster Hurricane Irene on Twitter.com. We collect over 65,000 Twitter messages relating to Hurricane Irene from August 18th to August 31st, 2011, and group them by location and gender. We train a sentiment classifier to categorize messages based on level of concern, and then use this classifier to investigate demographic differences. We report three principal findings: (1) the number of Twitter messages related to Hurricane Irene in directly affected regions peaks around the time the hurricane hits that region; (2) the level of concern in the days leading up to the hurricane's arrival is dependent on region; and (3) the level of concern is dependent on gender, with females being more likely to express concern than males. Qualitative linguistic variations further support these differences. We conclude that social media analysis provides a viable, real-time complement to traditional survey methods for understanding public perception towards an impending disaster.

Introduction

In 2011, natural disasters cost the United States more than 1,000 lives and $52 billion. The number of disasters costing over $1 billion in 2011 (twelve) is more than in the entire decade of the 1980s.[1] As the number of people living in disaster-prone areas grows, it becomes increasingly important to have reliable, up-to-the-minute assessments of emergency preparedness during impending disasters. Understanding issues such as personal risk perception, preparedness, and evacuation plans helps public agencies better tailor emergency warnings, preparations, and response.

Social scientists typically investigate these issues using polling data. The research shows significant demographic differences in response to government warnings, personal risk assessment, and evacuation decisions (Perry and Mushkatel, 1986; Perry and Lindell, 1991; Goltz et al., 1992; Fothergill et al., 1999; West and Orr, 2007; Enarson, 1998). For example, Fothergill et al. (1999) find that minorities differ in their risk perception and in their response to emergency warnings, with some groups having fatalistic sentiments that lead to greater fear and less preparedness. Goltz et al. (1992) find that people with lower income and education, Hispanics, and women all expressed greater fear of earthquakes.

This past research suggests governments could benefit by tailoring their messaging and response to address the variability between groups. While survey data have advanced our knowledge of these issues, they have two major drawbacks for use in disaster research. First, most surveys rely on responses to hypothetical scenarios, for example by asking subjects if they would evacuate under certain scenarios. This *hypothetical bias* is well-known (Murphy et al., 2005). Second, surveys are often impractical in disaster scenarios. In a rapidly-changing environment, governments cannot wait for a time-consuming survey to be conducted and the results analyzed before making warning and response decisions. Additionally, survey response rates shortly before or after a disaster are likely to be quite low, as citizens are either without power or are busy preparing or rebuilding. Thus, it is difficult to collect data

[1]"Record year for billion-dollar disasters", CBS News, December 7, 2011.

during the critical times immediately before and after the disaster.

In this paper, we investigate the feasibility of assessing public risk perception using social media analysis. Social media analysis has recently been used to estimate trends of interest such as stock prices (Gilbert and Karahalios, 2010), movie sales (Asur and Huberman, 2010), political mood (O'Connor et al., 2010a), and influenza rates (Lampos and Cristianini, 2010; Culotta, 2010; Culotta, 2012). We apply a similar methodology here to assess the public's level of concern toward an impending natural disaster.

As a case study, we examine attitudes toward Hurricane Irene expressed on Twitter.com. We collect over 65,000 Twitter messages referencing Hurricane Irene between August 18th and August 31st, 2011; and we train a sentiment classifier to annotate messages by level of concern. We specifically look at how message volume and sentiment varies over time, location, and gender.

Our findings indicate that message volume increases over the days leading up to the hurricane, and then sharply decreases following its dispersal. The timing of the increase and subsequent decrease in messages differs based on the location relative to the storm. There is also an increasing proportion of concerned messages leading up to Hurricane Irene's arrival, which then decreases after Irene dissipation. A demographic analysis of the proportion of concerned messages shows significant differences both by region and gender. The gender differences in particular are supported by previous survey results from the social science literature (West and Orr, 2007). These results suggest that social media analysis is a viable technology for understanding public perception during a hurricane.

The remainder of the paper is organized as follows: First, we describe the data collection methodology, including how messages are annotated with location and gender. Next, we present sentiment classification experiments comparing various classifiers, tokenization procedures, and feature sets. Finally, we apply this classifier to the entire message set and analyze demographic variation in levels of concern.

Data Collection

Irene became a tropical storm on August 20th, 2011, and hit the east coast of the United States between August 26th and 28th. This hurricane provides a compelling case to investigate for several reasons. First, Irene affected many people in many states, meaning that regional differences in responses can be investigated. Second, there was considerable media and political attention surrounding Hurricane Irene, leading to it being a popular topic on social network sites. Third, the fact that there was forewarning of the hurricane means that responses to it can be evaluated over time.

Twitter is a social networking site that allows users to post brief, public messages to their followers. Using Twitter's API[2], we can sample many messages as well as their meta-data, such as time, location, and user name. Also, since Twitter can be used on smart phones with batteries, power outages due to natural disasters will presumably have less of an effect on the volume of messages.

Using Twitter's sampling API ("spritzer"), we sample approximately uniformly from all messages between August 18 and August 31. We then perform keyword filtering to collect messages containing the words "Irene" or "Hurricane", or the hashtag "#Irene". During the period of August 18th to August 31st, messages containing these keywords are overwhelmingly related to Hurricane Irene and not some other event. This results in 65,062 messages.

Inferring Location

In order to determine the location of the message sender, we process the user-reported location data from that user's profile. Since not all users enter accurate location data, we search for specific keywords in order to classify the messages by state. For example, if the location data contains a token "VT" or "Vermont," it is labeled as coming from Vermont. (See Appendix A for more details.) The locations we consider are the 13 states directly affected by Hurricane Irene, plus Washington DC. These locations are then grouped into 3 regions. First, the New England region consists of the states of Connecticut, Massachusetts, Rhode Island, New Hampshire, Vermont, and Maine. Second, the Middle States region

[2]http://dev.twitter.com

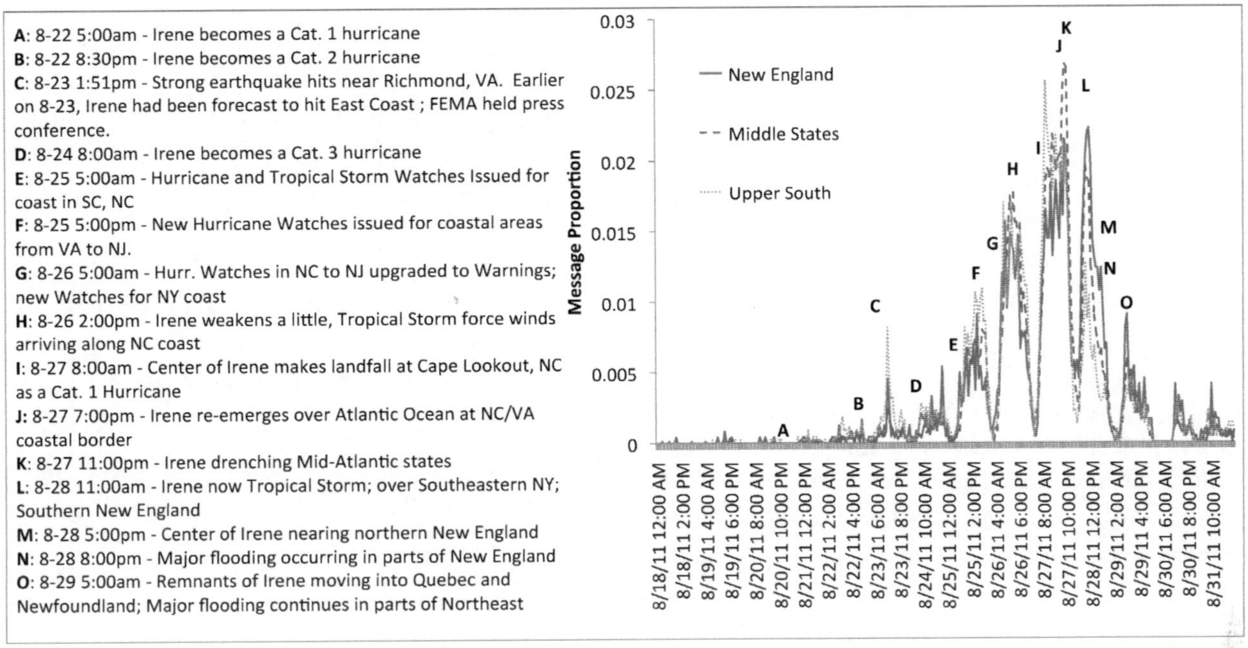

Figure 1: Results from Hurricane Irene Twitter data showing the influence of disaster-related events on the number of messages from each region. The y-axis is the proportion of all Irene-related messages from each region that were posted during each hour.

consists of New York, New Jersey, and Pennsylvania. Third, the Upper South region consists of North Carolina, Virginia, Maryland, Delaware, and Washington DC.

Of the messages that we collect between August 18th and August 31st, 15,721 are identified as belonging to one of the directly affected areas. Grouped into regions, we find that 2,424 are from New England, 8,665 are from the Middle-States region, and 4,632 are from the Upper South region.

Figure 1 displays the messages per hour from each of the three regions. The y-axis is normalized over all messages from that region — e.g., a value of 0.02 for New England means that 2% of all messages from New England over the 10 day span were posted in that hour. This allows us to see which time periods were the most active for that region. Indeed, we see that the spikes occur in geographical order of the hurricane's path, from the South, to the Mid-Atlantic region, and finally New England. Additionally, Figure 1 is marked with data points indicating which events were occurring at that time.

There are several obvious limitations of this approach (as explored in Hecht et al. (2011)). For example, users may enter false location information, have an outdated profile, or may be posting messages from a different location. Assuming these issues introduce no systemic bias, aggregate analyses should not be significantly impacted (as supported by the observed trends in Figure 1).

Inferring Gender

To determine the gender of the message sender, we process the name field from the user's profile obtained from the Twitter API. The U.S. Census Bureau provides a list of the most popular male and female names in the United States. The lists contain over 1,000 of the most common male names and over 4,000 of the most common female names. After removing names that can be either male or female (for example, Chris or Dana), we match the first name of the user to the list of names obtained from the census. Users that cannot be classified in such a manner are labeled as unsure. The data contains a total of 60,808 distinct users, of which 46% are assigned a gender (of those, 55% are female, 45% male). We find that many of the unlabeled users are news agencies. A similar methodology is used by Mislove et al. (2011). As with geographic inference,

Total Sample 8/18/2011-8/31/2011	25,253,444
Matching Irene Keywords	65,062
Female-indicative names	16,326
Male-indicative names	13,597
Mid-Atlantic states	8,665
Upper-South states	4,632
New England states	2,424

Table 1: Number of messages in sample for each filter.

we make no attempt to model any errors introduced by this process (e.g., users providing false names). Table 1 displays statistics of the overall dataset. A sample of 100 messages revealed no misattributed location or gender information.

Sentiment Classification

In this section, we describe experiments applying sentiment classification to assess the level of concern of each message. Our goal is not to investigate new sentiment classification techniques, but instead to determine whether existing, well-known methods are applicable to this domain. While there is an extensive literature in sentiment classification technology (Pang and Lee, 2008), binary classification using a bag-of-words assumption has been shown to provide a strong baseline, so that is the approach we use here. We also evaluate the impact of lexicons and tokenization strategies.

We define "concerned" messages to be those showing some degree of apprehension, fear, or general concern regarding Hurricane Irene. Examples of unconcerned messages include links to news reports or messages expressing an explicit lack of concern. The idea is to assess how seriously a particular group is reacting to an impeding disaster.

To train the classifier, we sample 408 messages from the 66,205 message collection and manually annotate them as concerned or unconcerned. The final training set contains 170 concerned messages. Examples are shown in Table 2. To estimate inter-annotator agreement, we had a second annotator sample 100 labeled messages (50 concerned, 50 unconcerned) for re-annotation. The inter-annotator agreement is 93% (Cohen's kappa $\kappa = .86$).

Examples of concerned messages
wonderful, praying tht this hurricane goes back out to sea.
Im actually scared for this hurricane...
This hurricane is freaking me out.
hope everyone is #safe during #irene
Examples of unconcerned messages
for the very latest on hurricane irene like our fb page ...
am i the only one who doesn't give a shit about this hurricane??
tropical storm irene's track threatens south florida - miamiherald.com

Table 2: Examples of concerned and unconcerned messages from the training set.

Tokenization and features

We train a simple bag-of-words classifier, where the basic feature set is the list of word frequencies in each message. Given the brevity and informality of Twitter messages, tokenization choices can have a significant impact on classification accuracy. We consider two alternatives:

- **Tokenizer0:** The tokenizer of O'Connor et al. (2010b), which does very little normalization. Punctuation is preserved (for the purpose of identifying semantics such as emoticons), URLs remain intact, and text is lower-cased.
- **Tokenizer1:** A simple tokenizer that removes all punctuation and converts to lowercase.

We also consider two feature pruning options:

- **Stop Words:** Remove words matching a list of 524 common English words.
- **Frequency Pruning:** Remove words occurring fewer than 2 times in the labeled data.

We also consider the following features:

- **Worry lexicon:** We heuristically create a small lexicon containing words expressing worry of some kind, based on a brief review of the data.[3] We replace all such tokens with a WORRIED feature.

[3]The words are afraid, anxiety, cautious, die, died, nervous, pray, prayers, prayin, praying, safe, safety, scared, scary, terrified, thoughts, worried, worry, worrying

Classifier	Acc	Pr	Re	F1
MaxEnt	**84.27 ± 2.0**	90.15	70.00	78.81
Dec. Tree	81.35 ± 1.8	79.72	67.06	72.84
Naive Bayes	78.63 ± 2.2	75.78	71.76	73.72
Worry Lex.	79.41	95.74	52.94	68.18

Table 3: Average accuracy (with standard error) and micro-averaged precision, recall, and F1 for the three sentiment classifiers, using their best configurations. The difference in accuracy between MaxEnt and the other classifiers is statistically significant (paired t-test, $p < 0.01$).

- **Humor lexicon:** Similarly, we create a small lexicon containing words expressing humor.[4] We replace all such tokens with a HUMOR feature.
- **Emoticon:** Two common emoticons ":)" and ":(" are detected (prior to tokenization in the case of Tokenizer 1).

Finally, we consider three classifiers: MaxEnt (i.e., logistic regression), Naive Bayes, and a Decision Tree (ID3) classifier, as implemented in the MALLET machine learning toolkit (McCallum, 2002). We use all the default settings, except we set the maximum decision tree depth to 50 (after preliminary results suggested that the default size of 4 was too small).

Enumerating the possible tokenization, features, and classifier choices results in 192 possible system configurations. For each configuration, 10-fold cross-validation is performed on the labeled training data. Table 3 reports the results for each classifier using its best configuration. The configuration Tokenizer1/Remove Stop Words/Freq. Pruning/Worry lexicon/Humor lexicon/Emoticons was the best configuration for both MaxEnt and Naive Bayes. Decision Tree differed only in that its best configuration did not use Frequency Pruning. Table 3 also compares to a simple baseline that classifies messages as concerned if they contain any of the words in the worry lexicon (while accuracy is competitive, recall is quite low).

MaxEnt exhibits the best accuracy, precision, and F1; Naive Bayes has slightly better recall. Table 4 provides a summary of the numerical impact each

[4] The words are lol, lmao, rofl, rotfl, ha, haha.

System Configuration	Avg Acc	Max Acc
Tokenizer0	77.78	81.10
Tokenizer1	80.59	84.27
Keep Stop Words	77.99	81.34
Remove Stop Words	80.38	84.27
No Freq. Pruning	79.67	83.29
Freq. Pruning	78.71	84.27
No Worry lexicon	77.62	81.82
Worry lexicon	80.76	84.27
No Humor Lexicon	79.15	83.78
Humor Lexicon	79.23	84.27
No Emoticons	79.26	84.27
Emoticons	79.11	84.27

Table 4: Summary of the impact of various tokenization and feature choices. The second and third columns list the average and maximum accuracy over all possible system configurations with that setting. All results use the MaxEnt classifier and 10-fold cross-validation. **Tokenizer1**, **Remove Stop Words**, and **Worry Lexicon** result in the largest improvements in accuracy.

configuration choice has. Using MaxEnt, we compute the accuracy over every possible system configuration, then average the accuracies to obtain each row. Thus, the Tokenizer1 row reports the average accuracy over all configurations that use Tokenizer1. Additionally, we report the highest accuracy of any configuration using that setting. These results indicate that Tokenizer1, Remove Stop Words, and Worry Lexicon result in the largest accuracy gains. Thus, while some unsupervised learning research has suggested that only light normalization should be used for social media text analysis (O'Connor et al., 2010b), for this supervised learning task it appears that more aggressive normalization and feature pruning can improve accuracy.

We select the best performing MaxEnt classifier for use in subsequent experiments. First we retrain the classifier on all the labeled data, then use it to label all of the unlabeled data from the original 65,062 messages. To estimate performance on this new data, we sample 200 additional documents of this testing data and manually label them (35 positive, 165 negative). We find that the automated classifications are accurate in 86% of these documents. Many of the remaining errors appear to be difficult cases. For example, consider the message: "1st an earthquake, now a hurricane? Damn NY do you miss me that bad?" The classifier labels this as concerned, but the message is likely intended to be humorous. In another message ("#PrayForNYC and everyone that will experience Hurricane Irene"), a hashtag #PrayForNYC complicates tokenization, so the word "pray" (highly correlated with concern) is not detected, resulting in a false negative.

Demographic Analysis

We next apply this classifier to assess the demographic determinants of concerned messages. By classifying all remaining messages, we can analyze trends in sentiment over time by gender and region.

Figure 2 displays the total number of messages by day as well as the subset (and percentage) that are classified as concerned. Consulting the timeline in Figure 1, we see that the peak volume occurs on August 27th, the day the eye of the hurricane makes landfall. The percentage of messages labeled as concerned actually peaks a day earlier, on August 26th.

Geographic Analysis

We first make several observations concerning Figure 1, which does not use the sentiment classifier, but only displays message volume. There appears to be a regional difference in when message volume peaks. Data point C in the figure, which marks the time around 2pm on August 23rd, represents the first noticeable spike in message count, particularly in the Upper South region. Two important events were occurring around this time period. First, the strongest earthquake to hit the Eastern United States since WWII (measured as 5.8 on the Richter scale) occurs near Richmond, Virginia. Also on August 23rd, a few hours prior to the earthquake, FEMA holds a press conference regarding the impeding threat that Hurricane Irene will pose to East Coast states. It appears likely that the combination of these events leads to the increase in messages on August 23rd as revealed in the figure. In fact, in examining some of the messages posted on Twitter during that time period, we notice some people commenting on the unlikeliness that two natural disasters would hit the region in such a narrow time frame.

Also in Figure 1, we see that the frequency of Twitter messages relating to Hurricane Irene for each region increases greatly over roughly the period of August 25th to August 28th, before decreasing later on August 28th and beyond. The increase and decrease roughly parallel the approach of Hurricane Irene toward and then beyond each region. Data point I represents the time (August 27th at 8am) when the center of Hurricane Irene makes landfall on the North Carolina coast. This point represents the highest message count for the Upper South region. Later on August 27th, as the hurricane moves north toward New Jersey and then New York, we see the peak message count for the Middle States region (Data point K). Finally, on August 28th in the late morning, as Hurricane Irene moves into the New England region, we see that the New England regions peak message count occurs (Data Point L).

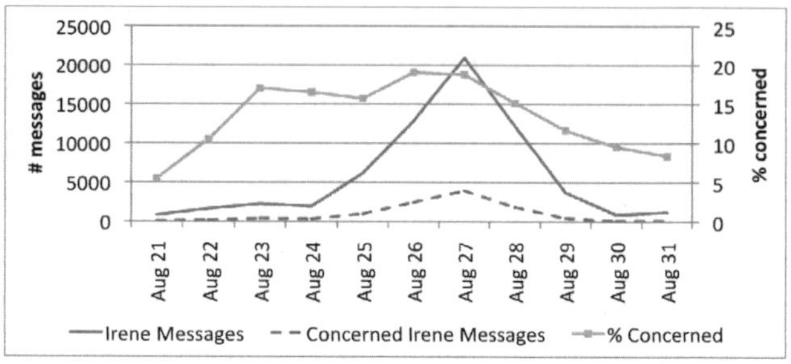

Figure 2: Total number of Twitter messages related to Hurricane Irene, as well as the count and percentage classified as *concerned* by the sentiment classifier.

With the sentiment classifier from the previous section, we can perform a more detailed analysis of the regional differences than can be performed using message volume alone. Figure 3 applies the sentiment classifier to assess the proportion of messages from each region that express concern. Figure 3 (top) shows the raw percentage of messages from each region by day, while the bottom figure shows the proportion of messages from each region that express concern. While the New England region has the lowest volume of messages, on many days it has the highest proportion of concerned messages.

Comparing regional differences in aggregate across all 10 days would be misleading – after the hurricane passes a region, it is expected that the level of concern should decrease. Indeed, these aggregate regional differences are not statistically significant (NE=15.59%, MID=15.4%, SOUTH=15.69%). Instead, for each day we compare the levels of concern

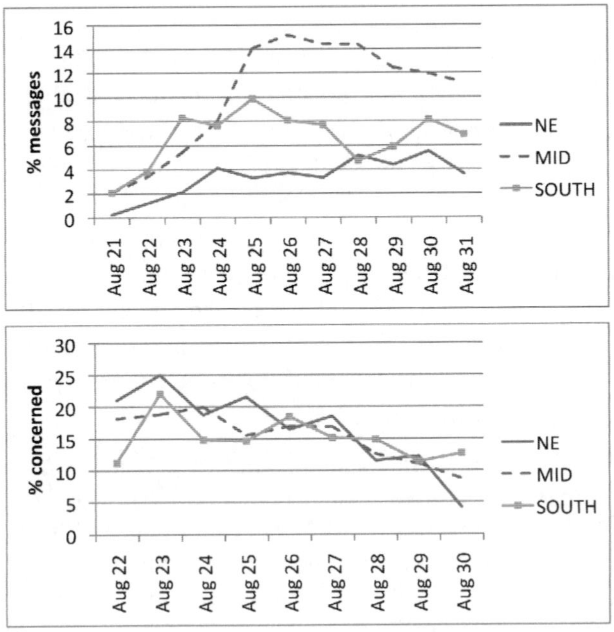

Figure 3: Message proportion and percent classified as concerned by the sentiment classifier, by region.

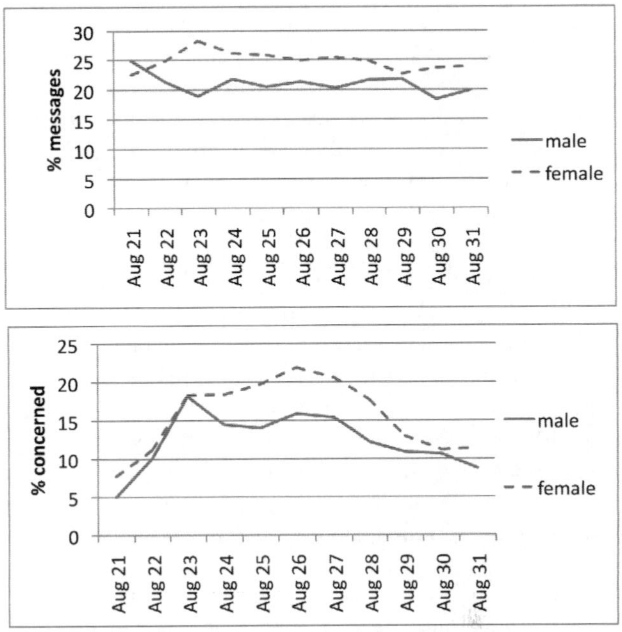

Figure 4: Message proportion and percent classified as concerned by the sentiment classifier, by gender.

for each region, testing for significance using a Chi-squared test. Two days show significant differences: August 25 and August 27. On both days, the proportion of concerned messages in New England is significantly higher ($p < 0.05$) than that of the Southern region (August 25: NE=21.6%, SOUTH=14.6%; August 26: NE=18.5%, SOUTH=15.1%). It is difficult to directly attribute causes to these differences, although on August 25, a Hurricane Watch was issued for the New England area, and on August 27 that Watch was upgraded to a Warning. It is also possible that states that experience hurricanes more frequently express lower levels of concern. Further sociological research is necessary to fully address these differences.

Gender Analysis

We apply a similar analysis to assess the differences in levels of concern by gender. Figure 4 shows that for roughly the period between August 24th and August 29th, messages written by females are more likely to express concern than those written by males. Over the entire period, 18.7% of female-authored messages are labeled as concerned, while over the same period 13.9% of male-authored messages are labeled as concerned. We perform a Chi-squared test over the entire period, and find that gender differences in concern are significant ($p < .01$). We conclude that messages attributed to female authors are significantly more likely to be classified as concerned than messages authored by males.

In order to assess a possible gender bias in our classifier, we examine the proportion of concern for males and females in the labeled training set. We find that of the original 408 labeled messages, 69 are from males, 112 are from females, and 227 cannot be determined. 24 male messages, or 34.8%, are marked as concerned. In contrast, 57 female messages, or 50.9%, are marked as concerned. 88 of the undetermined gender messages, or 38.9%, are concerned. We therefore down-sample the female messages from our labeled training set until the proportion of female-concerned messages matches that of male-concerned messages. Repeating our classification experiments shows no significant difference in the relative proportions of messages labeled as concerned by gender. We therefore conclude that the training set is not injecting a gender bias in the classifier.

Female: i my safe praying this everyone died jada butistillloveu brenda who love t me thank school pets retweet respects all please here so stay neverapologizefor wine sleep rainbow prayers lord
Male: http co de en el hurac media breaking la rooftoproofing track obama jimnorton gay ron blames smem change seattle orkaan becomes disaster zona zan lean vivo por es location dolphin
New England: boston MAirene ct vt ri england sunday connecticut malloy ma vermont tropical maine wtnh massachusetts haven rhode VTirene va power CThurricane cambridge mass lls gilsimmons mbta gunna storm slut NHirene
Middle States: nyc ny nj nycmayorsoffice york jersey mta brooklyn zone nytmetro va ryan philly shut dc mayor city manhattan lls new subways con team longisland bloomberg evacuation evacuate yorkers catskills queens
South: nc dc va lls earthquake raleigh maryland dmv ncwx virginia ncirene richmond isabelle perdue isabel mdhurricane bout carolina capitalweather sniper rva norfolk goin feeds nycmayorsoffice baltimore ilm mema tho aint

Table 5: Top 30 words for each demographic ranked by Information Gain.

Qualitative Analysis

In Table 5 we provide a brief qualitative analysis by displaying the top 30 words for each demographic obtained using Information Gain (Manning and Schtze, 1999), a method of detecting features that discriminate between document classes. To provide some of the missing context: “jada” refers to the divorce of celebrities Will Smith and Jada Pinkett; “hurac” refers to the Spanish word *Huracán*; “smem” stands for Social Media for Emergency Management; “dolphin” refers to a joke that was circulated referencing the hurricane; “lls” is an abbreviation for “laughing like shit”.

Some broad trends appear: male users tend to reference news, politics, or jokes; the Middle States reference the evacuation of New York City, and the South refers back to other disasters (the earthquake, the sniper attacks of 2002, Hurricane Isabel).

Related Work

Recent research has investigated the effectiveness of social media for crisis communication (Savelyev et al., 2011) — indeed, the U.S. Federal Emergency Management Agency now uses Twitter to disseminate information during natural disasters (Kalish, 2011). Other work has examined the spread of false rumors during earthquakes (Mendoza et al., 2010) and tsunamis (Acar and Muraki, 2011) and characterized social network dynamics during floods (Cheong and Cheong, 2011), fires (Vieweg et al., 2010), and violence (Heverin and Zach, 2010). While some of this past research organizes messages by topic, to our knowledge no work has analyzed disaster sentiment or its demographic determinants.

Survey research by West and Orr (2007) concluded that women may feel more vulnerable during hurricanes because they are more likely to have children and belong to a lower socio-economic class. Richer people, they find, tend to have an easier time dealing with natural disasters like hurricanes. These reasons might explain our finding that women are more likely on Twitter to show concern than men about Hurricane Irene. West and Orr also find differences in regional perceptions of vulnerability between coastal areas and non-coastal areas. Our location annotation must be more precise before we can perform a similar analysis.

More generally, our approach can be considered a type of *computational social science*, an emerging area of study applying computer science algorithms to social science research (Lazer et al., 2009; Hopkins and King, 2010).

Conclusion and Future Work

Our results show that analyzing Twitter messages relating to Hurricane Irene reveals differences in sentiment depending on a person’s gender or location. We conclude that social media analysis is a viable complement to existing survey methodologies, providing real-time insight into public perceptions of a disaster. Future directions include investigating how to account for classifier error in hypothesis testing (Fuller, 1987), adjusting classification proportions using quantification methods (Forman, 2007), as well as applying the approach to different disasters and identifying additional sentiment classes of interest. Finally, it will be important to infer a greater variety of demographic attributes and also to adjust for the demographic bias inherent in social media.

References

Adam Acar and Yuya Muraki. 2011. Twitter for crisis communication: lessons learned from Japan's tsunami disaster. *International Journal of Web Based Communities*, 7(3):392–402.

S. Asur and B. A. Huberman. 2010. Predicting the future with social media. In *Proceedings of the ACM International Conference on Web Intelligence*.

France Cheong and Christopher Cheong. 2011. Social media data mining: A social network analysis of tweets during the 2010–2011 Australian floods. In *PACIS 2011 Proceedings*.

Aron Culotta. 2010. Towards detecting influenza epidemics by analyzing Twitter messages. In *Workshop on Social Media Analytics at the 16th ACM SIGKDD Conference on Knowledge Discovery and Data Mining*.

Aron Culotta. 2012. Lightweight methods to estimate influenza rates and alcohol sales volume from Twitter messages. *Language Resources and Evaluation, Special Issue on Analysis of Short Texts on the Web*. to appear.

Elaine Enarson. 1998. Through women's eyes: A gendered research agenda for disaster social science. *Disasters*, 22(2):157–73.

George Forman. 2007. Quantifying counts, costs, and trends accurately via machine learning. Technical report, HP Laboratories, Palo Alto, CA.

A. Fothergill, E.G. Maestas, and J.D. Darlington. 1999. Race, ethnicity and disasters in the united states: A review of the literature. *Disasters*, 23(2):156–73, Jun.

W.A. Fuller. 1987. *Measurement error models*. Wiley, New York.

Eric Gilbert and Karrie Karahalios. 2010. Widespread worry and the stock market. In *Proceedings of the 4th International AAAI Conference on Weblogs and Social Media*, Washington, D.C., May.

J.D. Goltz, L.A. Russell, and L.B. Bourque. 1992. Initial behavioral response to a rapid onset disaster: A case study. *International Journal of Mass Emergencies and Disasters*, 10(1):43–69.

Brent Hecht, Lichan Hong, Bongwon Suh, and Ed H. Chi. 2011. Tweets from justin bieber's heart: the dynamics of the location field in user profiles. In *Proceedings of the 2011 annual conference on Human factors in computing systems*, CHI '11, pages 237–246, New York, NY, USA.

T. Heverin and L. Zach. 2010. Microblogging for crisis communication: Examination of Twitter use in response to a 2009 violent crisis in Seattle-Tacoma, Washington area. In *Proceedings of the Seventh International Information Systems for Crisis Response and Management Conference*, Seattle, WA.

Daniel J. Hopkins and Gary King. 2010. A method of automated nonparametric content analysis for social science. *American Journal of Political Science*, 54(1):229–247.

Brian Kalish. 2011. FEMA will use social media through all stages of a disaster. Next Gov, February.

Vasileios Lampos and Nello Cristianini. 2010. Tracking the flu pandemic by monitoring the social web. In *2nd IAPR Workshop on Cognitive Information Processing (CIP 2010)*, pages 411–416.

David Lazer, Alex Pentland, Lada Adamic, Sinan Aral, Albert-Laszlo Barabasi, Devon Brewer, Nicholas Christakis, Noshir Contractor, James Fowler, Myron Gutmann, Tony Jebara, Gary King, Michael Macy, Deb Roy, and Marshall Van Alstyne. 2009. Computational social science. *Science*, 323(5915):721–723.

Chris Manning and Hinrich Schtze. 1999. *Foundations of Statistical Natural Language Processing*. MIT Press, Cambridge, MA, May.

Andrew Kachites McCallum. 2002. MALLET: A machine learning for language toolkit. http://mallet.cs.umass.edu.

Marcelo Mendoza, Barbara Poblete, and Carlos Castillo. 2010. Twitter under crisis: Can we trust what we RT? In *1st Workshop on Social Media Analytics (SOMA '10)*, July.

Alan Mislove, Sune Lehmann, Yong-Yeol Ahn, Jukka-Pekka Onnela, , and J. Niels Rosenquist. 2011. Understanding the demographics of twitter users. In *Proceedings of the Fifth International AAAI Conference on Weblogs and Social Media (ICWSM'11)*, Barcelona, Spain.

James Murphy, P. Allen, Thomas Stevens, and Darryl Weatherhead. 2005. A meta-analysis of hypothetical bias in stated preference valuation. *Environmental and Resource Economics*, 30(3):313–325.

Brendan O'Connor, Ramnath Balasubramanyan, Bryan R. Routledge, and Noah A. Smith. 2010a. From Tweets to polls: Linking text sentiment to public opinion time series. In *International AAAI Conference on Weblogs and Social Media*, Washington, D.C.

Brendan O'Connor, Michel Krieger, and David Ahn. 2010b. Tweetmotif: Exploratory search and topic summarization for twitter. In *ICWSM*.

Bo Pang and Lillian Lee. 2008. Opinion mining and sentiment analysis. *Foundations and Trends in Information Retrieval*, 2(1–2):1–135.

R.W. Perry and M.K. Lindell. 1991. The effects of ethnicity on decision-making. *International journal of mass emergencies and disasters*, 9(1):47–68.

R.W. Perry and A.H. Mushkatel. 1986. *Minority citizens in disasters*. University of Georgia Press, Athens, GA.

Alexander Savelyev, Justine Blanford, and Prasenjit Mitra. 2011. Geo-twitter analytics: Applications in crisis management. In *25th International Cartographic Conference*, pages 1–8.

Sarah Vieweg, Amanda L. Hughes, Kate Starbird, and Leysia Palen. 2010. Microblogging during two natural hazards events: what twitter may contribute to situational awareness. In *Proceedings of the 28th international conference on Human factors in computing systems*, pages 1079–1088, New York, NY, USA.

Darrell M. West and Marion Orr. 2007. Race, gender, and communications in natural disasters. *The Policy Studies Journal*, 35(4).

Appendix A: Location String Matching

The following strings were matched against the user location field of each message to determine the location of the message. Matches were case insensitive, except for abbreviations (e.g., VT must be capitalized to match).

Vermont, VT, Maine, ME, New Hampshire, Rhode Island, RI, Delaware, DE, Connecticut, CT, Maryland, MD, Baltimore, North Carolina, NC, Massachusetts, MA, Boston, Mass, W Virginia, West Virginia, Virginia, VA, RVA, DC, D.C., PA, Philadelphia, Pittsburgh, Philly, New Jersey, Atlantic City, New York, NY, NYC, Long Island, Manhattan, Brooklyn, Staten Island, The Bronx, Queens, NY, N.Y.

Detecting Influencers in Written Online Conversations

Or Biran[1]* **Sara Rosenthal[1]*** **Jacob Andreas[1]****

Kathleen McKeown[1]* **Owen Rambow[2]†**

[1] Department of Computer Science, Columbia University, New York, NY 10027
[2] Center for Computational Learning Systems, Columbia University, New York, NY 10027
* {orb, sara, kathy}@cs.columbia.edu
** jda2129@columbia.edu †rambow@ccls.columbia.edu

Abstract

It has long been established that there is a correlation between the dialog behavior of a participant and how influential he or she is perceived to be by other discourse participants. In this paper we explore the characteristics of communication that make someone an opinion leader and develop a machine learning based approach for the automatic identification of discourse participants that are likely to be influencers in online communication. Our approach relies on identification of three types of conversational behavior: persuasion, agreement/disagreement, and dialog patterns.

1 Introduction

In any communicative setting where beliefs are expressed, some are more influential than others. An influencer can alter the opinions of their audience, resolve disagreements where no one else can, be recognized by others as one who makes important contributions, and often continue to influence a group even when not present. Other conversational participants often adopt their ideas and even the words they use to express their ideas. These forms of *personal influence* (Katz and Lazarsfeld, 1955) are part of what makes someone an opinion leader. In this paper, we explore the characteristics of communication that make someone an opinion leader and develop a machine learning based approach for the automatic identification of discourse participants who are likely to be influencers in online communication.

Detecting influential people in online conversational situations has relevance to online advertising strategies which exploit the power of peer influence on sites such as Facebook. It has relevance to analysis of political postings, in order to determine which candidate has more appeal or which campaign strategy is most successful. It is also relevant for designing automatic discourse participants for online discussions ("chatbots") as it can provide insight into effective communication. Despite potential applications, analysis of influence in online communication is a new field of study in part because of the relatively recent explosion of social media. Thus, there is not an established body of theoretical literature in this area, nor are there established implementations on which to improve. Given this new direction for research, our approach draws on theories that have been developed for identifying influence in spoken dialog and extends them for online, written dialog. We hypothesize that an influencer, or an influencer's conversational partner, is likely to engage in the following conversational behaviors:

Persuasion: An influencer is more likely to express personal opinions with follow-up (e.g., justification, reiteration) in order to convince others.

Agreement/disagreement: A conversational partner is more likely to agree with an influencer, thus implicitly adopting his opinions.

Dialog Patterns: An influencer is more likely to participate in certain patterns of dialog, for example initiating new topics of conversation, contributing more to dialog than others, and engendering longer dialog threads on the same topic.

Our implementation of this approach comprises a system component for each of these conversational behaviors. These components in turn provide the features that are the basis of a machine learning approach for the detection of likely influencers. We test this approach on two different datasets, one drawn from Wikipedia discussion threads and the other drawn from LiveJournal weblogs. Our results show that the system performs better for detection of influencer on LiveJournal and that there are interesting differences across genres for detecting the different forms of conversational behavior.

The paper is structured as follows. After reviewing related work, we define influence, present our data and methods. We present a short overview of the black box components we use for persuasion and detection of agreement/disagreement, but our focus is on the development of the influencer system as a whole and thus we spend most time exploring the results of experimentation with the system on different data sets, analyzing which components have most impact. We first review related work.

2 Related Work

It has long been established that there is a correlation between the conversational behavior of a discourse participant and how influential he or she is perceived to be by the other discourse participants (Bales et al., 1951; Scherer, 1979; Brook and Ng, 1986; Ng et al., 1993; Ng et al., 1995). Specifically, factors such as frequency of contribution, proportion of turns, and number of successful interruptions have been identified as being important indicators of influence. Reid and Ng (2000) explain this correlation by saying that "conversational turns function as a resource for establishing influence": discourse participants can manipulate the dialog structure in order to gain influence. This echoes a starker formulation by Bales (1970): "To take up time speaking in a small group is to exercise power over the other members for at least the duration of the time taken, regardless of the content." Simply claiming the conversational floor is a feat of power. This previous work presents two issues for a study aimed at detecting influence in written online conversations.

First, we expect the basic insight – conversation as a resource for influence – to carry over to written dialog: we expect to be able to detect influence in written dialog as well. However, some of the characteristics of spoken dialog do not carry over straightforwardly to written dialog, most prominently the important issue of interruptions: there is no interruption in written dialog. Our work draws on findings for spoken dialog, but we identify characteristics of written dialog which are relevant to influence.

Second, the insistence of Bales (1970) that power is exercised through turn taking "regardless of content" may be too strong. Reid and Ng (2000) discuss experiments which address not just discourse structure features, but also a content feature which represents how closely a turn is aligned with the overall discourse goal of one of two opposing groups (with opposing opinions on a specific issue) participating in the conversation. They show that interruptions are more successful if aligned with the discourse goal. They propose a model in which such utterances "lead to participation which in turn predicts social influence", so that the correlation between discourse structure and influence is really a secondary phenomenon. However, transferring such results to other types of interactions (for example, in which there are not two well-defined groups) is challenging. In this study, we therefore examine two types of features as they relate to influence: content-related (persuasion and agreement/disagreement), and discourse structure-related.

So far, there has been little work in NLP related to influencers. Quercia et al. (2011) look at influencers' language use in Twitter contrasted to other users' groups and find some significant differences. However, their analysis and definition relies quite heavily on the particular nature of social activity on Twitter. Rienks (2007) discusses detecting influencers in a corpus of conversations. While he focuses entirely on non-linguistic behavior, he does look at (verbal) interruptions and topic initiations which can be seen as corresponding to some of our Dialog Patterns Language Uses.

3 What is an Influencer?

Our definition of an influencer was collectively formulated by a community of researchers involved in the IARPA funded project on Socio Cultural Content in Language (SCIL).

This group defines an influencer to be someone who:

P1 by Arcadian $<pc_1>$There seems to be a much better list at the National Cancer Institute than the one we've got.$</pc_1><pa_1>$It ties much better to the actual publication (the same 11 sections, in the same order).$</pa_1>$ I'd like to replace that section in this article. Any objections?
P2 by JFW $<pc_2><a_1>$Not a problem.$</a_1></pc_2>$Perhaps we can also insert the relative incidence as published in this month's wiki Blood journal
P3 by Arcadian I've made the update. I've included template links to a source that supports looking up information by ICD-O code.
P4 by Emmanuelm Can Arcadian tell me why he/she included the leukemia classification to this lymphoma page? It is not even listed in the Wikipedia leukemia page! $<pc_3>$I vote for dividing the WHO classification into 4 parts in 4 distinct pages: leukemia, lymphoma, histocytic and mastocytic neoplasms.$</pc_3><pa_3>$ Remember, Wikipedia is meant to be readable $</pa_3>$by all. Let me know what you think before I delete the non-lymphoma parts.
P5 by Arcadian Emmanuelm, aren't you the person who added those other categories on 6 July 2005?
P6 by Emmanuelm $<d_1>$Arcadian, I added only the lymphoma portion of the WHO classification. You added the leukemias on Dec 29th.$</d_1>$Would you mind moving the leukemia portion to the leukemia page?
P7 by Emmanuelm $<pc_4>$Oh, and please note that I would be very comfortable with a "cross-coverage" of lymphocytic leukemias in both pages.$</pc_4>$My comment is really about myeloid, histiocytic and mast cell neoplasms who share no real relationship with lymphomas.
P8 by Arcadian $<pa_5><a_2>$To simplify the discussion, I have restored that section to your version. $</a_2></pa_5>$You may make any further edits, and $<pc_6>$I will have no objection.$</pc_6>$
P9 by JFW The full list should be on the hematological malignancy page, and the lymphoma part can be here. $<pc_7>$It would be defendable to list ALL and CLL here.$</pc_7><pa_7>$They fall under the lymphoproliferative disorders.$</pa_7>$

Table 1: Influence Example: A Wikipedia discussion thread displaying Emmanuelm as the influencer. Replies are indicated by indentation (for example, P2 is a response to P1). All Language Uses are visible in this example: Attempt to Persuade ($\{pc_i, pa_i\}$), Claims (pc_i), Argumentation (pa_i), Agreement (a_i), Disagreement (d_i), and the five Dialog Patterns Language Uses (eg. Arcadian has positive Initiative).

1. Has credibility in the group.
2. Persists in attempting to convince others, even if some disagreement occurs
3. Introduces topics/ideas that others pick up on or support.

By *credibility*, we mean someone whose ideas are adopted by others or whose authority is explicitly recognized. We hypothesize that this shows up through agreement by other conversants. By *persists*, we mean someone who is able to eventually convince others and often takes the time to do so, even if it is not quick. This aspect of our definition corresponds to earlier work in spoken dialog which shows that frequency of contributions and proportion of turns is a method people use to gain influence (Reid and Ng, 2000; Bales, 1970). By point 3, we see that the influencer may be influential even in directing where the conversation goes, discussing topics that are of interest to others. This latter feature can be measured through the discourse structure of the interaction. The influencer must be a group participant but need not be active in the discussion(s) where others support/credit him.

The instructions that we provided to annotators included this definition as well as examples of who is *not* an influencer. We told annotators that if someone is in a hierarchical power relation (e.g., a boss), then that person is not an influencer to sub-ordinates (or, that is not the type of influencer we are looking for). We also included someone with situational power (e.g., authority to approve other's actions) or power in directing the communication (e.g., a moderator) as negative examples.

We also gave positive examples of influencers. Influencers include an active participant who argues against a disorganized group and resolves a discussion is an influencer, a person who provides an answer to a posted question and the answer is accepted after discussion, and a person who brings knowledge to a discussion. We also provided positive and negative examples for some of these cases.

Table 1 shows an example of a dialog where there is evidence of influence, drawn from a Wikipedia Talk page. A participant (Arcadian) starts the thread with a proposal and a request for support from other participants. The influencer (Emmanuelm) later joins the conversation arguing against Arcadian's proposal. There is a short discussion, and Arcadian defers to Emmanuelm's position. This is one piece of dialog within this group where Emmanuelm may demonstrate influence. The goal of our system is to find evidence for situations like this, which suggests that a person is more likely to be an influencer.

Since we attempt to find local influence (a person who is influential in a particular thread, as opposed to influential in general), our notion of influencer is consistent with diverse views on social influence. It is consistent with the definition of influencer proposed by Gladwell (2001) and Katz (1957): an exceptionally convincing and influential person, set apart from everyone else by his or her ability to spread opinions. While it superficially seems inconsistent with Duncan Watts' concept of "accidental influentials" (Watts, 2007), that view does not make the assertion that a person cannot be influential in a particular situation (in fact, it predicts that someone will) - only that one cannot in general identify people who are always more likely to be influencers.

4 Data and Annotation

Our data set consists of documents from two different online sources: weblogs from LiveJournal and discussion forums from Wikipedia.

LiveJournal is a virtual community in which people write about their personal experiences in a weblog. A LiveJournal entry is composed of a post (the top-level content written by the author) and a set of comments (written by other users and the author). Every comment structurally descends either from the post or from another comment.

Each article on Wikipedia has a discussion forum (called a Talk page) associated with it that is used to discuss edits for the page. Each forum is composed of a number of threads with explicit topics, and each thread is composed of a set of posts made by contributors. The posts in a Wikipedia discussion thread may or may not structurally descend from other posts: direct replies to a post typically descend from it. Other posts can be seen as descending from the topic of the thread.

For consistency of terms, from here on we refer to each weblog or discussion forum thread as a *thread* and to each post or comment as a *post*.

We have a total of 333 threads: 245 from LiveJournal and 88 from Wikipedia. All were annotated for influencers. The threads were annotated by two undergraduate students of liberal arts. These students had no prior training or linguistic background. The annotators were given the full definition from section 3 and asked to list the participants that they thought were influencers. Each thread may in principle have any number of influencers, but one or zero influencers per thread is the common case and the maximal number of influencers found in our dataset was two. The inter-annotator agreement on whether or not a participant is an influencer (given by Cohen's Kappa) is 0.72.

5 Method

Our approach is based on three conversational behaviors which are identified by separate system components described in the following three sections. Figure 1 shows the pipeline of the Influencer system and Table 1 displays a Wikipedia discussion thread where there is evidence of an influencer and in which we have indicated the conversational behaviors as they occur. Motivated by our definition, each component is concerned with an aspect of the likely influencer's discourse behavior:

Persuasion examines the participant's language to identify attempts to persuade, such as $\{pc_1, pa_1\}$ in Table 1, which consist of claims (e.g. pc_1) made by the participant and supported by argumentations (e.g. pa_1). It also identifies claims and argumentations independently of one another (pc_4 and pa_5).

Agreement/Disagreement examines the other participants' language to find how often they agree or disagree with the participant's statements. Examples are a_1 and d_1 in Table 1.

Dialog Patterns examines how the participant interacts in the discussion structurally, independently of the content and the language used. An example of this is Arcadian being the first poster and contributing the most posts in the thread in Table 1.

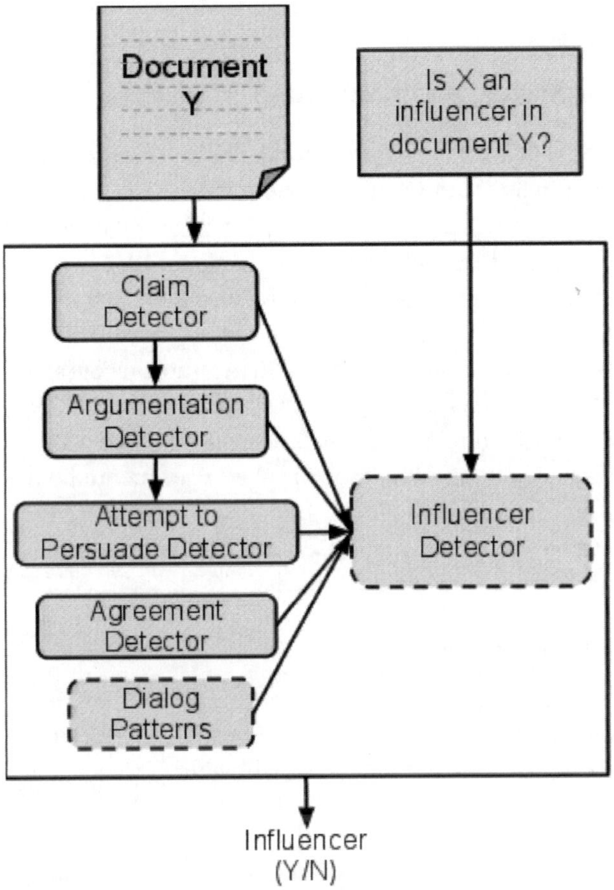

Figure 1: The influencer pipeline. Solid lines indicate black-box components, which we only summarize in this paper. Dashed lines indicate components described here.

Each component contributes a number of *Language Uses* which fall into that category of conversational behavior and these Language Uses are used directly as features in a supervised machine learning model to predict whether or not a participant is an influencer. For example, Dialog Patterns contributes the Language Uses *Initiative*, *Irrelevance*, *Incitation*, *Investment* and *Interjection*.

The Language Uses of the Persuasion and Agreement/Disagreement components are not described in detail in this paper, and instead are treated as black boxes (indicated by solid boxes in Figure 1). We have previously published work on some of these (Biran and Rambow, 2011; Andreas et al., 2012). The remainder of this section describes them briefly and provides the results of evaluations of their performance (in Table 2). The next section describes the features of the Dialog Patterns component.

5.1 Persuasion

This component identifies three Language Uses: Attempt to Persuade, Claims and Argumentation.

We define an attempt to persuade as a set of contributions made by a single participant which may be made anywhere within the thread, and which are all concerned with stating and supporting a single claim. The subject of the claim does not matter: an opinion may seem trivial, but the argument could still have the structure of a persuasion.

Our entire data set was annotated for attempts to persuade. The annotators labeled the text participating in each instance with either *claim*, the stated opinion of which the author is trying to persuade others or *argumentation*, an argument or evidence that supports that claim. An attempt to persuade must contain exactly one claim and at least one instance of argumentation, like the {claim, argumentation} pairs $\{pc_1, pa_1\}$ and $\{pc_3, pj_3\}$ in Table 1.

In addition to the complete *attempt to persuade* Language Use, we also define the less strict Language Uses *claims* and *argumentation*, which use only the subcomponents as stand-alones.

Our work on argumentation, which builds on Rhetorical Structure Theory (Mann and Thompson, 1988), is described in (Biran and Rambow, 2011).

5.2 Agreement/Disagreement

Agreement and disagreement are two Language Uses that model others' acceptance of the participant's statements. Annotation (Andreas et al., 2012) is performed on pairs of phrases, $\{p_1, p_2\}$. A phrase is a substring of a post or comment in a thread. The annotations are directed since each post or comment has a time stamp associated with it. This means that p_1 and p_2 are not interchangeable. p_1 is called the "target phrase", and p_2 is called the "subject phrase". A person cannot agree with him- or herself, so the author of p_1 and p_2 cannot be the same. Each annotation is also labeled with a type: either "agreement" or "disagreement".

6 Dialog Patterns

The Dialog Patterns component extracts features based on the structure of the thread. Blogs and discussion threads have a tree structure, with a blog post or a topic of discussion as the root and a set of

Component	Wikipedia			LiveJournal		
	P	R	F	P	R	F
Attempt to persuade	79.1	69.6	74	57.5	48.2	52.4
Claims	83.6	74.5	78.8	53.7	13.8	22
Argumentation	23.3	91.7	37.1	30.9	48.9	37.8
Agreement	12	31.9	17.4	20	50	28.6
Disagreement	8.7	9.5	9.1	6.3	14.3	8.7

Table 2: Performance of the black-box Language Uses in terms of Precision (P), Recall (R), and F-measure(F).

Conversational Behavior Component	Language Use (Feature)	Users		
		A	J	E
Persuasion	Claims	2/6	2/6	2/6
	Argumentation	Y	Y	Y
	Attempt to Persuade	Y	Y	Y
Agreement/ Disagreement	Agreement	1/1	0/1	0/1
	Disagreement	1/1	0/1	0/1
Dialog Patterns	Initiative	Y	N	N
	Irrelevance	2/4	1/2	1/3
	Incitation	4	1	3
	Interjection	1/9	2/9	4/9
	Investment	4/9	2/9	3/9

Table 3: The feature values for each of the participants, Arcadian (A), JFW (J), and Emmanuelm (E), in the Wikipedia discussion thread shown in Table 1.

comments or posts which are marked as a reply - either to the root or to an earlier post. The hypothesis behind Dialog Patterns is that influencers have typical ways in which they participate in a thread and which are visible from the structure alone.

The Dialog Patterns component contains five simple Language Uses:

Initiative The participant is or is not the first poster of the thread.

Irrelevance The percentage of the participant's posts that are not replied to by anyone.

Incitation The length of the longest branch of posts which follows one of the participant's posts. Intuitively, the longest discussion started directly by the participant.

Investment The participant's percentage of all posts in the thread.

Interjection The point in the thread, represented as percentage of posts already posted, at which the participant enters the discussion.

7 System and Evaluation

The task of the system is to decide for each participant in a thread whether or not he or she is an influencer in that particular thread. It is realized with a supervised learning model: we train an SVM with a small number of features, namely the ten Language Uses. One of our goals in this work is to evaluate which Language Uses allow us to more accurately classify someone as an influencer. Table 3 shows the full feature set and feature values for the sample discussion thread in Table 1. We experimented with a number of different classification methods, including bayesian and rule-based models, and found that SVM produced the best results.

7.1 Evaluation

We evaluated on Wikipedia and LiveJournal separately. The data set for each corpus consists of all participants in all threads for which there was at least one influencer. We exclude threads for which no influencer was found, narrowing our task to finding the influencers where they exist. For each participant X in each thread Y, the system answers the following question: *Is X an influencer in Y?*

We used a stratified 10-fold cross validation of each data set for evaluation, ensuring that the same participant (from two different threads) never appeared in both training and test at each fold, to eliminate potential bias from fitting to a particular participant's style. The system components were identical when evaluating both data sets, except for the claims system which was trained on sentiment-annotated data from the corpus on which it was evaluated.

Table 4 shows the performance of the full system and of systems using only one Language Use feature compared against a baseline which always answers positively (X is always an influencer in Y). It also shows the performance for the best system, which was found for each data set by looking at all possible combinations of the features. The best system for the Wikipedia data set is composed of four features: Claims, Argumentation, Agreement and Investment. The best LiveJournal system is composed of all five Dialog Patterns features, Attempt to Persuade and Argumentation. We found our results to be statis-

System	Wikipedia			LiveJournal		
	P	R	F	P	R	F
Baseline: all-yes	16.2	100	27.9	19.2	19.2	32.2
Full	40.5	80.5	53.9	61.7	82	70.4
Initiative	31.6	31.2	31.4	73.5	72.7	73.1
Irrelevance	21.7	77.9	34	19.2	100	32.2
Incitation	28.3	77.9	41.5	49.5	73.8	59.2
Investment	43	71.4	53.7	50.2	75.4	60.3
Interjection	24.7	88.3	38.6	36.9	91.3	52.5
Agreement	36	46.8	40.7	45.1	82.5	58.3
Disagreement	35.3	70.1	47	19.2	100	32.2
Claims	40	72.7	51.6	54.3	76	63.3
Argumentation	19	98.7	31.8	31.1	85.2	45.6
Attempt to persuade	23.7	79.2	36.5	37.4	48.1	42.1
Best system	**47**	**80.5**	**59.3**	**66.2**	**84.7**	**74.3**

Table 4: Performance in terms of Precision (P), Recall (R), and F-measure (F) using the baseline (everyone is an influencer), all features (full), individual features one at a time, and the best feature combination for each data set.

System	Wikipedia			LiveJournal		
	P	R	F	P	R	F
Baseline	13.9	100	24.5	14.2	100	24.9
Full	36.7	79.2	50.2	46.3	79.8	58.6
Best	40.1	76.6	52.7	48.2	81.4	60.6

Table 5: Performance on the data set of all threads, including those with no influencers. The 'Best System' is the system that performed best on the filtered data set.

Data Set	Our System			Gold Answers		
	P	R	F	P	R	F
Wikipedia	23.6	69.4	35.2	23.8	81.6	36.9
LiveJournal	37.5	48.1	42.1	40.7	61.8	49

Table 6: Performance of the Attempt to Persuade component in directly predicting influencers. A comparison of our system and the component's gold annotation. These experiments were run on the full data set, which is why the system results are not exactly those of Table 4.

tically significant (with the Bonferroni adjustment) in paired permutation tests between the best system, the full system and the baseline of each data set.

When we first performed these experiments, we used all threads in the data set. The performance on this full set was lower, as shown in Table 5 due to the presence of threads with no influencers. Threads in which the annotators could not find a clear influencer tend to be of a different nature: there is either no clear topic of discussion, or no argument (everyone is in agreement). We leave the task of distinguishing these threads from those which are likely to have an influencer to future work.

7.2 Evaluating with Perfect Components

In a hierarchical system such as ours, errors can be attributed to imperfect components or to a bad choice of features, so it is important to look at the potential contribution of the components. As an example, Table 6 shows the difference between our Attempt to Persuade system and a hypothetical perfect Attempt to Persuade component, simulated by using the gold annotations, when predicting influencer directly (i.e., a participant is an influencer iff she makes an attempt to persuade).

Clearly, when predicting influencers, Attempt to Persuade is a stronger indicator in LiveJournal than it is in Wikipedia. However, as shown in Table 2, our Attempt to Persuade system performs better on Wikipedia. This situation is reflected in Table 6, where the lower quality of the system component in LiveJournal corresponds to a significantly lower performance when applied to the influencer task. These results demonstrate that Attempt to Persuade is a good feature: a more precise feature value means higher predictability of influencer. In the future we will perform similar analyses for the other features.

8 Discussion

We evaluated our system on two corpora - LiveJournal and Wikipedia discussions - which differ in structure, context and discussion topics. As our results show, they also differ in the way influencers behave and the way others respond to them. To illustrate the differences, we contrast the sample Wikipedia thread (Table 1) with an example from LiveJournal (Table 7).

It is common in LiveJournal for the blogger to be an influencer, as is the case in our example thread, because the topic of the thread is set by the blogger and comments are typically made by her friends. This fact is reflected in our results: Initiative is a very strong indicator in LiveJournal, but not so in

P1 by poconell <pc_1>He really does make good on his promises! </pc_1><pa_1>Day three in office, and the Global Gag Rule (A.K.A"The Mexico City Policy") is gone!</pa_1>I was holding my breath, hoping it wouldn't be left forgotte. He didn't wait. <pc_2>He can see the danger and risk in this policy, and the damage it has caused to women and families.</pc_2><pc_3>I love that man!</pc_3>
P2 by thalialunacy <a_1>I literally shrieked 'HELL YES!' in my car when I heard. :D:D:D</a_1>
P3 by poconell <a_2>Yeah, me too</a_2>
P4 by lunalovepotter <pc_4><a_3>He is SO AWESOME!</a_3></pc_4><pa_4>Right down to business, no ifs, ands, or buts! :D</pa_4>
P5 by poconell <pc_5>It's amazing to see him so serious too!</pc_5><pa_5>This is one tough, no-nonsense man!</pa_5>
P6 by penny_sieve My icon says it all :)
P7 by poconell <pc_6>And I'm jealous of you with that President!</pc_6><pa_6>We tried to overthrow our Prime Minister, but he went crying to the Governor General. </pa_6>

Table 7: Influence Example: A LiveJournal discussion thread displaying poconell as the influencer. All the Language Uses are visible in this example: agreement/disagreement (a_i/d_i), persuasion ($\{pc_i, pa_i\}, pc_i, pa_i$), and dialog patterns (eg. poconell has positive Initiative). This example is very different from the Wikipedia example in Table 1.

Wikipedia, where the discussion is between a group of editors, all of whom are equally interested in the topic. In general, the Dialog Patterns features are stronger in LiveJournal. We believe this is due to the fact that the tree structure in LiveJournal is strictly enforced. In Wikipedia, people do not always reply directly to the relevant post. Investment is the exception: it does not make use of the tree structure, and is therefore an important indicator in Wikipedia.

Attempt to Persuade is useful in LiveJournal (the influencer poconell makes three attempts to persuade in Table 7) but less so in Wikipedia. This is explained by the precision of the gold system in Table 6. Only 23.8% of those who attempt to persuade in Wikipedia are influencers, compared with 40.7% in LiveJournal. Attempts to Persuade are more common in Wikipedia (all participants attempt to persuade in Table 1), since people write there specifically to argue their opinion on how the article should be edited. Conversely, agreement is a stronger predictor of influence in Wikipedia than in LiveJournal; we believe that is because of a similar phenomenon, that people in LiveJournal (who tend to know each other) agree with each other more often. Disagreement is not a strong indicator for either corpus which may say something about influencers in general - they can be disagreed with as often as anyone else.

9 Conclusion and Future Work

We have studied the relevance of content-related conversational behavior (persuasion and agreement/disagreement), and discourse structure-related conversational behavior to detection of influence. Identifying influencers is a hard task, but we are able to show good results on the LiveJournal corpus where we achieve an F-measure of 74.3%. Despite a lower performance on Wikipedia, we are still able to significantly outperform the baseline which yields only 28.2%. Differences in performance between the two seem to be attributable in part to the more straightforward dialog structure in LiveJournal.

There are several areas for future work. In our current work, we train and evaluate separately for our two corpora. Alternatively, we could investigate different training and testing combinations: train on one corpus and evaluate on the other; a mixed corpus for training and testing; genre-independent criteria for developing different systems (e.g. length of thread). We will also evaluate on new genres (such as the Enron emails) in order to gain an appreciation of how different genres of written dialog are.

Acknowledgment

This work has been supported by the Intelligence Advanced Research Projects Activity (IARPA) via Army Research Laboratory (ARL) contract number W911NF-09-C-0141. The U.S. Government is authorized to reproduce and distribute reprints for Governmental purposes notwithstanding any copyright annotation thereon.

References

Jacob Andreas, Sara Rosenthal, and Kathleen McKeown. 2012. Annotating agreement and disagreement in threaded discussion. In *Proceedings of the 8th International Conference on Language Resources and Computation (LREC)*, Istanbul, Turkey, May.

R. F. Bales, Strodtbeck, Mills F. L., T. M., and M. Roseborough. 1951. Channels of communication in small groups. *American Sociological Review*, pages 16(4), 461–468.

R. F. Bales. 1970. Personality and interpersonal behaviour.

Or Biran and Owen Rambow. 2011. Identifying justifications in written dialog. In *Proceedings of the Fifth IEEE International Conference on Semantic Computing*.

M.E. Brook and S. H. Ng. 1986. Language and social influence in small conversational groups. *Journal of Language and Social Psychology*, pages 5(3), 201–210.

Malcolm Gladwell. 2001. *The tipping point: how little things can make a big difference*. Abacus.

Elihu Katz and Paul F. Lazarsfeld. 1955. *Personal influence*. Free Press, Glencoe, IL. by Elihu Katz and Paul F. Lazarsfeld. With a foreword by Elmo Roper. "A report of the Bureau of Applied Social Research, Columbia University." Bibliography: p. 381-393.

E. Katz. 1957. *The Two-Step Flow of Communication: An Up-To-Date Report on an Hypothesis*. Bobbs-Merrill Reprint Series in the Social Sciences, S137. Ardent Media.

William C. Mann and Sandra A. Thompson. 1988. Rhetorical structure theory: Toward a functional theory of text organization. *Text*, 8(3):243–281.

S. H. Ng, D. Bell, and M. Brooke. 1993. Gaining turns and achieving high in influence ranking in small conversational groups. *British Journal of Social Psychology*, pages 32, 265–275.

S. H. Ng, M Brooke, and M. Dunne. 1995. Interruption and in influence in discussion groups. *Journal of Language and Social Psychology*, pages 14(4),369–381.

Daniele Quercia, Jonathan Ellis, Licia Capra, and Jon Crowcroft. 2011. In the mood for being influential on twitter. In *SocialCom/PASSAT*, pages 307–314. IEEE.

Scott A. Reid and Sik Hung Ng. 2000. Conversation as a resource for in influence: evidence for prototypical arguments and social identification processes. *European Journal of Social Psychology*, pages 30, 83–100.

Rutger Joeri Rienks. 2007. *Meetings in smart environments : implications of progressing technology*. Ph.D. thesis, Enschede, the Netherlands, July.

K. R. Scherer. 1979. Voice and speech correlates of perceived social influence in simulated juries. In *H. Giles and R. St Clair (Eds), Language and social psychology*, pages 88–120. Oxford: Blackwell.

Duncan Watts. 2007. The accidental influentials. *Harvard Business Review*.

Re-tweeting from a Linguistic Perspective

Aobo Wang **Tao Chen** **Min-Yen Kan**
Web IR / NLP Group (WING)
National University of Singapore
13 Computing Link, Singapore 117590
{wangaobo,taochen,kanmy}@comp.nus.edu.sg

Abstract

What makes a tweet worth sharing? We study the content of tweets to uncover linguistic tendencies of shared microblog posts (retweets), by examining surface linguistic features, deeper parse-based features and Twitter-specific conventions in tweet content. We show how these features correlate with a functional classification of tweets, thereby categorizing people's writing styles based on their different intentions on Twitter. We find that both linguistic features and functional classification contribute to re-tweeting. Our work shows that opinion tweets favor originality and pithiness and that update tweets favor direct statements of a tweeter's current activity. Judicious use of #hashtags also helps to encourage retweeting.

1 Introduction

Tweeting[1] is a modern phenomenon. Complementing short message texting, instant messaging, and email, tweeting is a public outlet for netizens to broadcast themselves. The short, informal nature of tweets allows users to post often and quickly react to others' posts, making Twitter an important form of close-to-real-time communication.

Perhaps as a consequence of its usability, form, and public nature, tweets are becoming an important source of data for mining emerging trends and opinion analysis. Of particular interest are retweets, tweets that share previous tweets from others. Tweets with a high retweet count can be taken as a first cut towards trend detection.

It is known that social network effects exert marked influence on re-tweeting (Wu et al., 2011; Recuero et al., 2011). But what about the content of the post? To the best of our knowledge, little is known about what properties of tweet content motivate people to share. Are there content signals that mark a tweet as important and worthy of sharing?

To answer these questions, we delve into the data, analyzing tweets to better understand posting behavior. Using a classification scheme informed by previous work, we annotate 860 tweets and propagate the labeling to a large 9M corpus (Section 2). On this corpus, we observe regularities in emoticon use, sentiment analysis, verb tense, named entities and hashtags (Section 3), that enable us to specify feature classes for re-tweet prediction. Importantly, the outcome of our analysis is that a single holistic treatment of tweets is suboptimal, and that re-tweeting is better understood with respect to the specific function of the individual tweet. These building blocks allow us to build a per-function based re-tweet predictor (Section 4) that outperforms a baseline.

2 Linguistically Motivated Tweet Classification

Before we can label tweets for more detailed classification, we must decide on a classification scheme. We first study prior work on tweet classification before setting off on creating our own classification for linguistic analysis.

This research is supported by the Singapore National Research Foundation under its International Research Centre Singapore Funding Initiative and administered by the IDM Programme Office, under grant 252-002-372-490.

[1] More generally known as microblogging, in which the post is termed a microblog.

Early ethnographic work on tweets manually created classification schemes based on personal, direct observation (Java et al., 2009; Kelly, 2009). Other work is more focused, aiming to use their constructed classification scheme for specific subsequent analysis (Naaman et al., 2010; Sriram et al., 2010; Ramage et al., 2010; Chen et al., 2010). All schemes included a range of 5–9 categories, and were meant to be exhaustive. They exhibit some regularity: all schemes included categories for information sharing, opinions and updates. They vary on their classification's level of detail and the intent of the classification in the subsequent analysis.

Most closely related to our work, Naaman et al. (2010) focused on distinguishing salient user activity, finding significant differences in posts about the tweeting party or about others that were reported by manually classifying tweets into nine categories, sampled from selected users. However, while their paper gave a useful classification scheme, they did not attempt to operationalize their work into an automated classifier.

Other works have pursued automated classification. Most pertinent is the work by Sriram et al. (2010), who applied a Naïve Bayes learning model with a set of 8 features (author ID, presence of shortened words, "@username" replies, opinionated words, emphasized words, currency and percentage signs and time phrases) to perform hard classification into five categories. To identify trending topics, Zubiaga et al. (2011) performed a similar classification, but at the topic level (as opposed to the individual tweet level) using aggregated language-independent features from individual tweets. Ramage et al. (2010) introduced four salient dimensions of tweets – style, status, social, substance. Individual terms and users were characterized by these dimensions, via labeled LDA, in which multiple dimensions could be applied to both types of objects.

While the previous work provides a good overview of the genre and topic classification of tweets, their analysis of tweets have been linguistically shallow, largely confined to word identity and Twitter-specific orthography. There has been no work that examines the discoursal patterns and content regularities of tweets. Understanding microblog posts from a deeper linguistic perspective may yield insight into the latent structure of these posts, and be useful for trend prediction. This is the aim of our work.

2.1 Classification Scheme

We hypothesize that people's intentions in posting tweets determine their writing styles, and such intentions can be characterized by the content and linguistic features of tweets. To test this hypothesis, we first collect a corpus of manually annotated tweets and then analyze their regularities. In constructing our classification annotation scheme, we are informed by the literature and adopt a two-level approach. Our coarser-grained Level-1 classification generalization is an amalgam of the schemes in Naaman et al. and Sriram et al.'s work; while our finer-grained, Level-2 classification further breaks down the Update and Opinion classes, to distinguish linguistic regularities among the subclasses. The left two columns of Table 1 list the categories in our scheme, accompanied by examples.

2.2 Dataset Collection

We collected three months of public tweets (from July to September in 2011) through Twitter's streaming API[2]. Non-English tweets were removed using regular expressions, incurring occasional errors. We note that tweets containing URLs are often spam tweets or tweets from automated services (e.g., Foursquare location check-ins) (Thomas et al., 2011), and that any retweet analysis of such tweets would need to focus much more on the linked content rather than the tweet's content. We thus removed tweets containing URLs from our study. While this limits the scope of our study, we wanted to focus on the (linguistic quality of) content alone. The final dataset explicitly identifies 1,558,996 retweets (hereafter, *RT-data*) and 7,989,009 non-retweets. To perform further analysis on Twitter hashtags (i.e., "#thankyousteve"), we break them into separate words using the Microsoft Data-Driven Word-Breaking API[3]. This also benefits the classification task in terms of converting hashtags to known words.

[2] `http://dev.twitter.com/docs/streaming-api`

[3] `http://web-ngram.research.microsoft.com/info/break.html`

Table 1: Our two-level classification with example tweets.

Level-1	Level-2	Motivation	Example retweets	Corpus count (%)
Opinion	*Abstract*	Present opinions towards abstract objects.	God will lead us all to the right person for our lives. Have patience and trust him.	291 (33.8%)
	Concrete	Present opinions towards concrete objects.	i feel so bad for nolan. Cause that poor kid gets blamed for everything, and he's never even there.	99 (11.5%)
	Joke	Tell jokes for fun.	Hi. I'm a teenager & I speak 3 languages: English, Sarcasm, & Swearing (; #TeenThings	86 (10.0%)
Update	*Myself*	Update my current status.	first taping day for #growingup tomorrow! So excited. :)	168 (19.6%)
	Someone	Update others' current status.	My little sister still sleep ...	66 (7.7%)
Interaction		Seek interactions with others.	#Retweet If you're #TeamFollowBack	81 (9.4%)
Fact		Transfer information.	Learnt yesterday: Roman Empire spent 75% of GDP on infrastructure. Roads, aqueducts, etc.	23 (2.7%)
Deals		Make deals.	Everybody hurry! Get to Subway before they stop serving LIMITED TIME ONLY item 'avocados'.	29 (3.4%)
Others		Other motivations.	Ctfu Lmfao At Kevin Hart ;)	17 (2.0%)

We employed U.S.-based workers on Amazon's Mechanical Turk to annotate a random subset of the preprocessed tweets. We collected annotations for 860 tweets (520 retweets; 340 non-retweets) randomly sampled from the final dataset, paying 10 cents per block of 10 tweets labeled. Each tweet was labeled by 3 different workers who annotated using the Level-2 scheme. Gold standard labels were inferred by majority. Inter-annotator agreement via Fleiss' κ showed strong (0.79) and modest (0.43) agreement at Level-1 and Level-2, respectively.

Table 1's rightmost columns illustrate the distribution of the annotated tweets on each category. From our Level-1 classification, *Opinion*, *Update* and *Interaction*, make up the bulk of the tweets in the annotated sample set. The remaining categories of *Facts*, *Deals* and *Others* make up only 8.1% in total. We thus focus only on the three major groups.

2.3 Labeled LDA Classification

Given the labeled data, we first observed that tweets in different classes have different content and language usage patterns. For example, tweets belonging to *Opinion* display more of an argumentative nature, exhibiting a higher use of second person pronouns (e.g., "you", "your"), modal verbs (e.g., "can", "could", "will", "must"), and particular adverbs (e.g., "almost", "nearly") than the other two groups. These observations lead us to employ the classifier that make use of words' co-occurrence feature to categorize tweets.

Hence, we adopt Labeled LDA, which extends Latent Dirichlet Allocation (LDA) (Blei et al., 2003) by incorporating supervision at the document level (here, tweet-level), enabling explicit models of text content associated with linguistic features. In adopting this methodology, we follow (Ramage et al., 2009) previous work on tweet classification. Features are encoded as special tokens to not overlap the tokens from the tweet content.

Tweets arguing in one style tend to share similar linguistic features. For example in Table 1, *Update* talks about ongoing events using present tense; and *Opinion* uses conjunctions to compose and connect ideas. To discover how people talk differently across genres of tweets, we extract five sets of linguistic features from each tweet, namely *Tense*[4], *Discourse Relations*[5], *Hashtags*, *Named Entities*[6], and *Interaction Lexical Patterns*[7].

We use default parameter settings for Labeled LDA. All the combinations of features were tested to find the best performing feature set. Table 2 quantifies the contribution of each feature and demonstrate the result from the best combination, as measured by Weighted Average F-Measure (WAFM). Compared to the performance of using baseline feature set using tweet content alone, the use of linguistic features improve the performance accordingly, with the exception of the use of named entities which reduced performance slightly, and hence was removed from the final classifier's feature set.

[4]Using the OpenNLP toolkit.

[5]Using (Lin et al., 2010)'s parser.

[6]Using the UW Twitter NLP tools (Ritter et al., 2011).

[7]Defined as Boolean matches to the following regular expressions: *"RT @[username]..."*, *"...via @[username]..."*, *"Retweeting @[username]..."*, *"Follow me if..."*, *"retweet @[username]..."*, *"...RT if..."* and *"Retweet if..."*

Scheme	C	CI	CT	CD	CH	CE	CITDH
Level-1	.625	.642	.635	.637	.629	.611	.670
Level-2	.413	.422	.427	.432	.415	.409	.451

Table 2: Weighted average F-measure results for the labeled LDA classification. Legend: C: tweet context; I: *Interaction*; T: *Tense*; D: *Discourse Relations*; H: *Hashtags*; E: *Named Entities*.

Require: Training set L; Test collection C; Evaluation set E; Iteration count I

function incrementalTraining(L,C,E,)

```
M ← labeledLDATraining(L)
e ← evaluate(M,E)
for c_i∈C and i < I do
    r_i ← predictLabel(c_i,M)
    r_selected ←pickItemsWithHighConfidence(r_i);
    L' ← add(r_selected) into L
    M' ← retrainLDAModel(L')
    e' ← evaluate(M',E)
    if e' is better than e then M ← m'; e ← e';
    else return M
    i ← i + 1
    keepLog(e')
return M
```

Figure 1: Pseudocode for incremental training.

2.4 Automated Classification

Starting with the best performing model trained on the *Level-1* schema (the CITDH feature set), we automatically classified the remaining tweets, using the incremental training algorithm described in Figure 1. The 860 annotated tweets were randomly split into a training set L and evaluation set E with a 5:1 ratio. The 9M unannotated tweets form the test collection C. c_i is assigned by randomly selecting 1000 tweets from C. I is computed as the size of C divided by the size of c_i. Note that retraining becomes more expensive as the dataset L' grows. Thus, we greedily generate a locally-optimal model, which completes after 6 iterations.

From the result of automatically labeled dataset, we see that the *Opinion* dominates the collection in count (44.6%), followed by *Interaction* (28.4%) and *Update* (20.5%). This result partially agrees with the manual classification results in Naaman et al. (2010), but differs in their *Information Sharing* category, which is broken down here as *Facts*, *Deals* and *Others*. We believe the discrepancies are due to the differences between the two datasets used. Their retweets were sampled from selected users who are active participants, and did not include tweets from organizations, marketers and dealers; in our case, the tweets are generally sampled without constraints.

3 Analysis of Linguistic Features

We now dissect retweets using the 1.5M *RT-data* defined in Section 2.2. We do this from a linguistic perspective, based on observations on the values and correlations among the features used for the automatic classification.

3.1 Emoticons and Sentiment

Emoticons such as smilies – :) – and frownies – : (– and their typographical variants, are prevalent in tweets. Looking at the distribution of emoticons, we find that 2.88% of retweets contain smilies and 0.26% contain frownies. In other words, smileys are used more often than frownies.

To give an overall picture of how sentiment is distributed among retweets, we employed the *Twitter Sentiment* Web API service (Go et al., 2009) to obtain polarity. Figure 2 shows that while neutral tweets dominate in all three classes, there are more negative tweets in the *Interaction* than in the other two. Such negative interactive comments usually find their use in sharing negative experiences in a dialogue or with their followers. *"Yeah I hate talking IN my phone. RT @Jadon Don't you guys hate talking in the phone"* is a representative example.

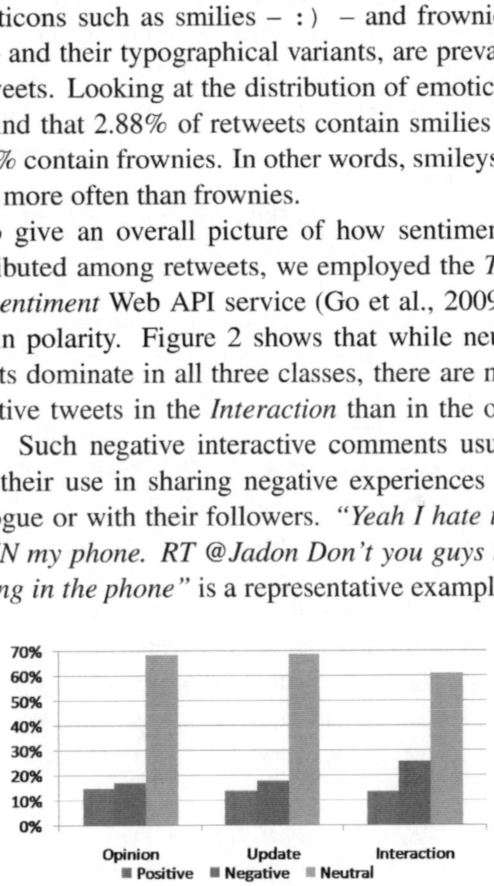

Figure 2: Sentiment distribution of retweets.

Previous works have leveraged emoticons to automatically build corpora for the sentiment detection task, through labeling tweets with smilies (frownies) as true positive (negative) instances (Read, 2005; Alexander and Patrick, 2010; Cui et al., 2011), and training statistical classification models on the result. We wish to verify the veracity of this hypothesis. Do emoticons actually reflect sentiment in

Table 3: Manual sentiment annotation results and confusion matrix. Bolded numbers highlight the error caused by neutral posts.

	Positive	Neutral	Negative
Retweets with smilies	55 (27.5%)	**140 (70%)**	5 (2.5%)
Retweets with frownies	9 (4.5%)	**118 (59%)**	73(36.5%)
Predicted Positive	43	**30**	0
Predicted Neutral	11	206	12
Predicted Negative	7	**29**	62

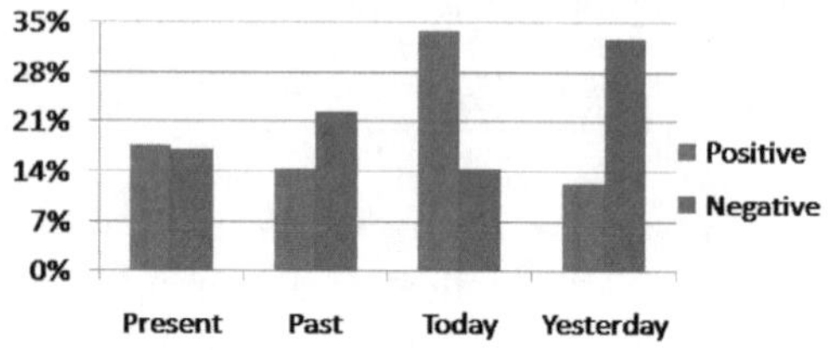

Figure 3: Tenses (l) and specific times (r) and their sentiment.

retweets? To answer the question, we randomly subselected 200 retweets with smilies and another 200 with frownies from *RT-data*, and then manually labeled their sentiment class after removing the emoticons. Table 3's top half shows the result.

While our experiment is only indicative, neutral posts are still clearly the majority, as indicated by bold numbers. Simply labeling the sentiment based on emoticons may mistake neutral posts for emotional ones, thus introducing noise into training data. *"Fishers people have no idea how lawrence kids are, guess they do now :)"* is such an example.

To demonstrate this effect, we evaluated Go et al. (2009)'s API on our annotated corpus. We present the confusion matrix in bottom half of Table 3. A common error is in mistaking neutral tweets as positive or negative ones, as indicated by the bold numbers. Given that the detector is trained on the corpus, in which neutral tweets with smiles (frownies) are labeled as positive (negative) ones, the detector may prefer to label neutral tweets as sentiment-bearing. This observation leads us to believe that more careful use of emoticons could improve sentiment prediction for tweets and microblog posts.

3.2 Verb Tense

We analyze the tense of the verbs in retweets, using a simplified inventory of tenses. We assign two tenses to verbs: past and present. Tense is assigned per-sentence; tweets that consist of multiple sentences may be assigned multiple tenses. Based on our statistics, one notable finding is that *Update* has a higher proportion of past tense use (33.70%) than *Opinion* (14.9%) and *Interaction* (24.2%). This validates that updates often report past events and verb tense is a more crucial feature for *Updates*.

Building on the previous section, we ask ourselves whether sentiment is correlated with verb tense use. Interestingly, the results are not uniform. Figure 3 shows our analysis of positive and negative (omitting neutral) sentiments as they co-occur with verb tense in our corpus. It shows that people tend to view the past negatively (e.g., *"I dont regret my past, I just regret the times I spent with the wrong people"*), whereas emotions towards current event do not have any obvious tendency. A case in point is in the use of "*today*" and "*yesterday*" as time markers related to present and past use. Figure 3 shows the number of tweets exhibiting these two words and their sentiment. The results are quite marked: tweets may be used to complain about past events, but look optimistically about things happening now.

3.3 Named Entities

To study the diversity of named entities (NEs) in retweets, we used UW Twitter NLP Tools (Ritter et al., 2011) to extract NEs from *RT-data*. 15.9% of retweets contain at least one NE, indicating that NEs do play a large role in retweets.

So what types of NEs do people mention in their tweets? From each of our primary Level-1 classes, we selected the top 100 correctly recognized NEs, in descending order of frequency. We then standardized variants (i.e. "*fb*" as a variant of "*Facebook*"), and manually categorized them against the 10-class schema defined by Ritter et al. (2011).

Table 4: The distribution of top 100 named entities[8].

Class	Opinion	Update	Interaction
PERSON	41.2%	44.7%	38.8%
GEO-LOC	7.8%	28.9%	25.4%
COMPANY	15.7%	6.6%	10.4%
PRODUCT	5.9%	5.3%	6.0%
SPORTS-TEAM	2.0%	5.3%	1.5%
MOVIE	7.8%	5.3%	7.5%
TV-SHOW	3.9%	0.0%	3.0%
OTHER	15.7%	3.9%	7.5%

Table 4 displays the distribution of the different classes of NEs, by frequency. People's names represent the largest portion in each class, of which the majority are celebrities. Geographical locations – either countries or cities – make up the second largest class for *Update* and *Interaction*, accounting for 28.9% and 25.4%, respectively, whereas they take only 7.8% of *Opinion*. A possible reason is that people prefer to broadcast about events (with locations mentioned) or discuss them through *Update* and *Interaction* classes, respectively. *"California, I'm coming home."* is a typical example.

3.4 Hashtags

Previous work (Cunha et al., 2011) showed that popular hashtags do share common characteristics, such as being short and simple. We want to push more in our analysis of this phenomenon. We organize our hashtag analysis around three questions: (a) Do people have any positional preference for embedding hashtags? (b) Are there any patterns to how people form hashtags? and (c) Is there any relationship between such patterns and their placement?

To answer these questions, as shown in Table 5, we extracted the hashtags from *RT-data* and categorized them by the position of their appearance (at the beginning, middle, or end) of tweet. 69.1% of hashtags occur at the end, 27.0% are embedded in the middle, and 8.9% occur at the beginning. In Figure 4, we plot the frequency and length (in characters) of the hashtags with respect to their position, which shows that the three placement choices lead to different distributions. Beginning hashtags (hereafter, beginners) tend to peak around a length of 11, while middlers peaked at around 7. Enders feature a bimodal distribution, favoring short (3) or longer (11+) lengths. We found these length distributions are artifacts of how people generate and (functionally) use the hashtags.

Beginners are usually created by concatenating the preceding words of a tweet, therefore, the common patterns are subject+verb (e.g.,*"#IConfess"*), subject+verb+object (e.g., *"#ucanthaveme"*), and similar variants. Middlers, often acting as a syntactic constituent in a sentence, are usually used to highlight tweet keywords, which are single-word nouns (e.g.,*"#Scorpio"* and *"#Dodgers"*). Enders provide additional information for the tweets. A popular ender pattern is Twitter slang that have been used enough to merit their own Twitter acronym, such as *"#TFB"* (Team Follow Back), and *"#TLT"* (Thrifty Living Tips). Another popular form is concatenating multiple words, indicating the time (*"#ToyaTuesday"*), the category (*"#Tweetyquote"*) or the location (*"#MeAtSchool"*). Knowing such hashtag usage can aid downstream applications such as hashtag suggestion and tweet search.

Table 5: Hashtags and example tweets.

Position	Tweets
Beginning	**#ihateitwhen** random people poke you on facebook
Middle	I just saw the **#Dodgers** listed on Craig's List.
End	Success is nothing without someone you love to share it with. **#TLT**
	Goodmorning Tweethearts....wishing u all blessed and productive day! **#ToyaTuesday**

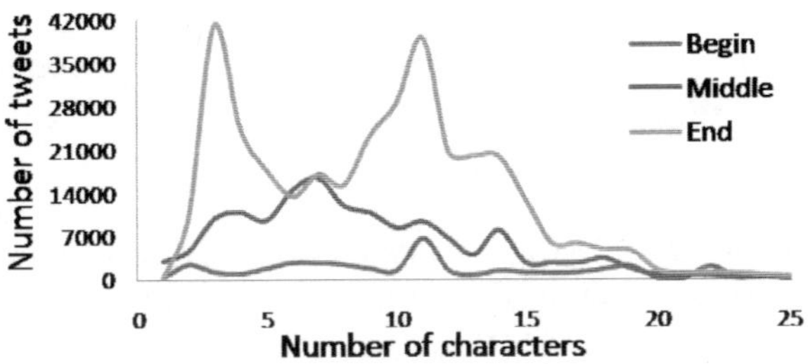

Figure 4: Length distribution of sampled hashtags.

3.5 Discourse Relations

In full text, textual units such as sentences and clauses work together to transmit information and give the discourse its argumentive structure. How important is discourse in the microblog genre, given its length limitation? To attempt an answer to this question, we utilized the end-to-end discourse parser proposed by Lin et al. (2010) to extract PDTB-styled discourse relations (Prasad et al., 2008) from *RT-data*. Figure 5 shows the proportion of the five most frequent relations. 68.0% of retweets had at least one discourse relation – per class, this was 55.2% of *Opinion*, 44.7% of *Interaction*, and 21.6% of *Update*. Within *Opinions*, we find that negative opinions are often expressed using a *Synchrony* relation (i.e., negative tweet: *"I hate when I get an itch at a*

[8]The other two classes, *facility* and *band*, are not found in the top 100 NEs.

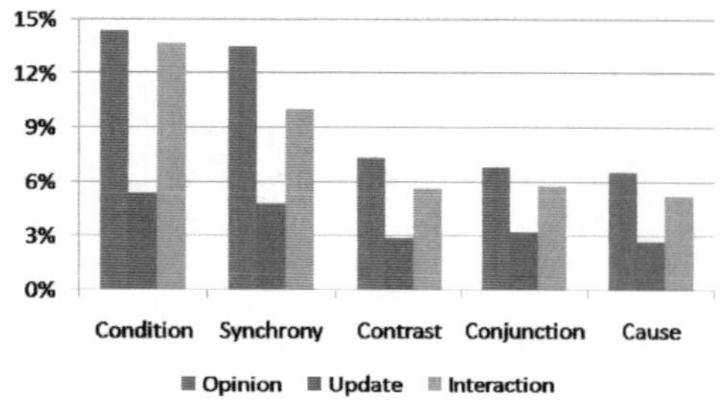

Figure 5: The distribution of five selected discourse relations.

place where my hand can't reach."), while positive and neutral opinions prefer *Condition* relations (i.e., positive tweet: "*If I have a girlfriend :) I will tell her beautiful everyday.*").

3.6 Sentence Similarity

"*On Twitter people follow those they wish they knew. On Facebook people follow those they used to know.*"

We round out our analysis by examining the sentence structure of retweets. Sometimes it is not what you say but on how you say it. This adage is especially relevant to the *Opinion* class, where we observed that the craftiness of a saying influences its "retweetability". This can be reflected in tweets having parallel syntactic structure, which can be captured by sentence similarity within a tweet, as illustrated in the quote/tweet above. We employ the *Syntactic Tree Matching* model proposed by Wang et al. (2009) on tweets to compute this value. This method computes tree similarity using a weighted version of tree kernels over the syntactic parse trees of input sentences. When we set the similarity threshold to 0.2 (determined by observation), 723 retweets are extracted from the *Opinion* class of which over 500 (70%) are among the top 5% most retweeted posts (by count). Examining this set reveals that they are more polarized (22.6% positive, 23.2% negative) than the average *Opinion* (14.7% and 16.9%, respectively).

4 Predicting Retweets

Given the diversity in function which we have illustrated in our linguistic analyses in the previous sections, we argue that whether a tweet is shared with others is best understood by modeling each function (Level-1) class independently. We validate this claim here, by showing how independently building classification models for the *Opinion*, *Update* and *Interaction* classes outperforms an agglomerated retweet predictor.

Previous research have found that features representing the author's profile (e.g., number of followers), tweet metadata (time interval between initial posting and current checkpoint, previously retweeted) and Twitter-specific features (URL presence) weight heavily in predicting retweets (Suh et al., 2010; Peng et al., 2011; Hong et al., 2011). In contrast, our study is strictly about the content and thus asks the question whether retweeting can be predicted from the content alone.

Before we do so, we call attention to a caveat about retweet prediction that we feel is important and unaccounted for in previous work: the actual probability of retweet is heavily dependent on how many people view the tweet. Twitter tracks the follower count of the tweet's author, which we feel is the best approximation of this. Thus we do not perform retweet count prediction, but instead cast our task as:

Given the content of a tweet, perform a multi-class classification that predicts its range of retweet per follower (RTpF) ratio.

4.1 Experiment and Results

We first examine RTpF distribution over the 9M tweets in the dataset. Figure 6 plots RTpF rank against retweet count on both normal and log-log scales. While the normal scale seems to show a typical exponential curve, the log-log scale reveals a clear inflection point that corresponds to an RTpF of 0.1. We use this inflection point to break the predicted RTpF values into three ordinal classes: no retweets ("N", RTpF = 0), low ("L", RTpF < 0.1), and high ("H", RTpF ≥ 0.1).

We use 10-fold cross validation logistic regression in Weka3 (Hall et al., 2009) to learn prediction models. The regression models use both binary presence-of feature classes (quotation; past, present tense; 16 types of discourse relations; 10 NE types; 3 hashtag positions) as well as normalized numeric features (tweet length, hashtag count, sentence similarity, 3 sentiment polarity strengths). Note that the models reported here do not factor the content (lexi-

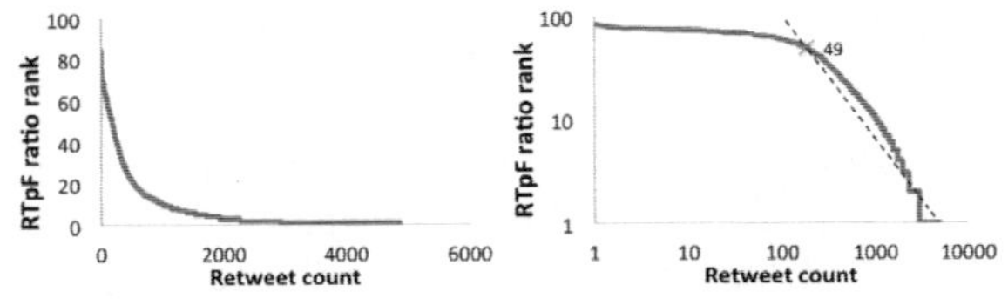

(a) Normal scale (b) Logarithmic scale

Figure 6: Retweet per follower (RTpF) ratio rank versus retweet count. The highlighted point shows the boundary between classes H and L.

Class	F_1	Salient Features	Feature Weight
Opinion	0.57	Sentence Similarity	10.34
		Conjunction	-21.09
		Quotation	-19.2
Update	0.54	Sentence Similarity	-2.81
		Past	-5.2
		Present	1.3
Interaction	0.53	Sentence Similarity	-55.33
		Hashtag Count	5.34
All w/ L-1 class	0.52	Sentence Similarity	9.8
All w/o L-1 class	0.42	Hashtag Count	22.03

Table 6: Logistic regression results. Salient features also shown with their respective weight, where a +ve value denotes a +ve contribution to retweet volume.

cal items) directly, but represent content through the lens of the feature classes given.

We build individual regression models for the three major Level-1 classes, and aggregate models that predict RTpF for all three classes. The two aggregate models differ in that one is informed of the Level-1 class of the tweets, while the other is not. We report average F-measure in Table 6 over the three RTpF classes ("N", "L" and "H"). Adding the Level-1 classification improves the RTpF prediction result by 10% in terms of average F_1. This results validate our hypothesis – we see that building separate logistic models for each class improves classification results uniformly for all three classes.

4.2 Remarks

We make a few conjectures based on our observations, in concluding our work:

1. Getting your *Opinion* retweeted is easier when your readership feels a sense of originality, pithiness and wittiness in your post. "*If you obey all the rules, you miss all the fun - Katharine Hepburn*" exemplifies these factors at conflict: while being witty in exhibiting parallel syntactic structure (high sentence similarity), it has a low RTpF. Perhaps followers are unsurprised when they find such beautiful words are not originally the poster's. Tweets having complex conjoined components and multiple clauses also exhibit a negative RTpF tendency – find a short and simple way of getting your message across.

2. *Update* tweets show the least bias towards any particular feature, exhibiting little weight towards any one convention. Update tweets prefer simple tenses, eschewing perfect and progressive variants. Perhaps followers are more curious about what you are doing now but not what you have done.

3. Sentence similarity negatively affects retweeting among *Interaction* tweets. This implies that people prefer direct sounds to well-designed proverbs in the daily interaction, which is mostly in the form of question answering or voting.

4. Globally, the presence and count of hashtags is correlated with retweeting, but this effect is greatly lessened when Level-1 class features are used. This further validates the importance of our functional classification of tweets.

5 Conclusion

People tweet for different reasons. Understanding the function of the tweet is interesting in its own right, but also useful in predicting whether it will be shared with others. We construct a two-level classification informed by prior work and have annotated a corpus of 860 tweets.

Employing Labeled LDA, we propagated our annotations to a large 9M tweet corpus and investigated the linguistic characteristics of the 1.5M retweets. We created a model to predict the level of retweeting per follower given a tweet's content.

Finally, to further encourage investigation on these topics, we have made the annotated corpus and the two tools described in this paper – the functional classifier and the retweet predictor – available to the public to test and benchmark against[9].

In future work, we plan to combine the content analysis from this study with known social, time and linked URL features to see whether content features can improve a holistic model of retweeting.

[9] `http://wing.comp.nus.edu.sg/tweets/`

References

Pak Alexander and Paroubek Patrick. 2010. Twitter as a corpus for sentiment analysis and opinion mining. In *Proceedings of the Seventh International Conference on Language Resources and Evaluation (LREC'10)*. European Language Resources Association (ELRA).

David M. Blei, Andrew Y. Ng, Michael I. Jordan, and John Lafferty. 2003. Latent dirichlet allocation. *Journal of Machine Learning Research*, 3:2003.

Jilin Chen, Rowan Nairn, Les Nelson, Michael Bernstein, and Ed H. Chi. 2010. Short and tweet: Experiments on recommending content from information streams. In *CHI 2010*.

Anqi Cui, Min Zhang, Yiqun Liu, and Shaoping Ma. 2011. Emotion tokens: Bridging the gap among multilingual twitter sentiment analysis. In *AIRS*, volume 7097 of *Lecture Notes in Computer Science*, pages 238–249. Springer.

Evandro Cunha, Gabriel Magno, Giovanni Comarela, Virgilio Almeida, Marcos André Gonçalves, and Fabricio Benevenuto. 2011. Analyzing the dynamic evolution of hashtags on twitter: a language-based approach. In *Proceedings of the Workshop on Language in Social Media (LSM 2011)*, pages 58–65, Portland, Oregon, June. ACL.

Alec Go, Richa Bhayani, and Lei Huang. 2009. Twitter sentiment classication using distant supervision. Technical report, Stanford University.

Mark Hall, Eibe Frank, Geoffrey Holmes, Bernhard Pfahringer, Peter Reutemann, and Ian H. Witten. 2009. The weka data mining software: an update. *SIGKDD Explor. Newsl.*, 11(1):10–18, November.

Liangjie Hong, Ovidiu Dan, and Brian D. Davison. 2011. Predicting popular messages in twitter. In *Proceedings of the 20th international conference companion on World wide web*, WWW '11, pages 57–58, New York, NY, USA. ACM.

Akshay Java, Xiaodan Song, Tim Finin, and Belle Tseng. 2009. Why we twitter: An analysis of a microblogging community. In *Proceedings of WebKDD/SNA-KDD 2007*, volume 5439 of *LNCS*, pages 118–138.

Ryan Kelly. 2009. Twitter study august 2009: Twitter study reveals interesting results about usage. `http://www.pearanalytics.com/blog/wp-content/uploads/2010/05/Twitter-Study-August-2009.pdf`, August.

Ziheng Lin, Hwee Tou Ng, and Min-Yen Kan. 2010. A pdtb-styled end-to-end discourse parser. Technical report, School of Computing, National University of Singapore.

Mor Naaman, Jeffrey Boase, and Chih-Hui Lai. 2010. Is it really about me?: message content in social awareness streams. In *Proceedings of the 2010 ACM conference on Computer supported cooperative work*, CSCW '10, pages 189–192, New York, NY, USA. ACM.

Huan-Kai Peng, Jiang Zhu, Dongzhen Piao, Rong Yan, and Ying Zhang. 2011. Retweet modeling using conditional random fields. In *ICDM 2011 Workshop on Data Mining Technologies for Computational Collective Intelligence*.

Rashmi Prasad, Nikhil Dinesh, Alan Lee, Eleni Miltsakaki, Livio Robaldo, Aravind Joshi, and Bonnie Webber. 2008. The penn discourse treebank 2.0. In *Proceedings of LREC*.

Daniel Ramage, David Hall, Ramesh Nallapati, and Christopher D. Manning. 2009. Labeled lda: a supervised topic model for credit attribution in multi-labeled corpora. In *Proceedings of the 2009 Conference on Empirical Methods in Natural Language Processing*, EMNLP '09, pages 248–256, Stroudsburg, PA, USA. ACL.

Daniel Ramage, Susan Dumais, and Dan Liebling. 2010. Characterizing microblogs with topic models. *International AAAI Conference on Weblogs and Social Media*, 5(4):130–137.

Jonathon Read. 2005. Using emoticons to reduce dependency in machine learning techniques for sentiment classification. In *Proceedings of the ACL Student Research Workshop*, ACLstudent '05, pages 43–48, Stroudsburg, PA, USA. ACL.

Raquel Recuero, Ricardo Araujo, and Gabriela Zago. 2011. How does social capital affect retweets? In Lada A. Adamic, Ricardo A. Baeza-Yates, and Scott Counts, editors, *ICWSM*. The AAAI Press.

Alan Ritter, Sam Clark, Mausam, and Oren Etzioni. 2011. Named entity recognition in tweets: An experimental study. In *Proceedings of the 2011 Conference on Empirical Methods in Natural Language Processing*, pages 1524–1534, Edinburgh, Scotland, UK., July. Association for Computational Linguistics.

Bharath Sriram, Dave Fuhry, Engin Demir, Hakan Ferhatosmanoglu, and Murat Demirbas. 2010. Short text classification in twitter to improve information filtering. In *Proceedings of the 33rd international ACM SIGIR conference on Research and development in information retrieval*, SIGIR '10, pages 841–842, New York, NY, USA. ACM.

Bongwon Suh, Lichan Hong, Peter Pirolli, and Ed H. Chi. 2010. Want to be retweeted? large scale analytics on factors impacting retweet in twitter network. In *Proceedings of the 2010 IEEE Second International Conference on Social Computing*, SOCIALCOM '10, pages 177–184, Washington, DC, USA. IEEE Computer Society.

Kurt Thomas, Chris Grier, Justin Ma, Vern Paxson, and Dawn Song. 2011. Design and evaluation of a real-time url spam filtering service. In *Proceedings of the 2011 IEEE Symposium on Security and Privacy*, SP '11, pages 447–462, Washington, DC, USA. IEEE Computer Society.

Kai Wang, Zhaoyan Ming, and Tat-Seng Chua. 2009. A syntactic tree matching approach to finding similar questions in community-based qa services. In *Proceedings of the 32nd international ACM SIGIR conference on Research and development in information retrieval*, SIGIR '09, pages 187–194, New York, NY, USA. ACM.

Shaomei Wu, Jake M. Hofman, Winter A. Mason, and Duncan J. Watts. 2011. Who says what to whom on twitter. In *Proceedings of the World Wide Web Conference*.

Arkaitz Zubiaga, Damiano Spina, Víctor Fresno, and Raquel Martínez. 2011. Classifying trending topics: a typology of conversation triggers on twitter. In *Proceedings of the 20th ACM international conference on Information and knowledge management*, CIKM '11, pages 2461–2464, New York, NY, USA. ACM.

Robust *kaomoji* detection in Twitter

Steven Bedrick, Russell Beckley, Brian Roark, Richard Sproat
Center for Spoken Language Understanding, Oregon Health & Science University
Portland, Oregon, USA

Abstract

In this paper, we look at the problem of robust detection of a very productive class of Asian style emoticons, known as facemarks or *kaomoji*. We demonstrate the frequency and productivity of these sequences in social media such as Twitter. Previous approaches to detection and analysis of *kaomoji* have placed limits on the range of phenomena that could be detected with their method, and have looked at largely monolingual evaluation sets (e.g., Japanese blogs). We find that these emoticons occur broadly in many languages, hence our approach is language agnostic. Rather than relying on regular expressions over a predefined set of likely tokens, we build weighted context-free grammars that reward graphical affinity and symmetry within whatever symbols are used to construct the emoticon.

1 Introduction

Informal text genres, such as email, SMS or social media messages, lack some of the modes used in spoken language to communicate affect – prosody or laughter, for example. Affect can be provided within such genres through the use of text formatting (e.g., capitalization for emphasis) or through the use of extra-linguistic sequences such as the widely used smiling, winking ;) emoticon. These sorts of vertical face representations via ASCII punctuation sequences are widely used in European languages, but in Asian informal text genres another class of emoticons is popular, involving a broader symbol set and with a horizontal facial orientation. These go by the name of facemarks or *kaomoji*. Figure 1 presents several examples of these sequences, including both relatively common *kaomoji* as well as more exotic and complex creations.

|^_^|	(๑•̂ت•̂๑)
[○_−]	(˘╎-˘╎ʅ)
\(^v^)/	(*≧m≦*)

Figure 1: Some representative *kaomoji* emoticons

This class of emoticon is far more varied and productive than the sideways European style emoticons, and even lists of on the order of ten thousand emoticons will fail to cover all instances in even a modest sized sample of text. This relative productivity is due to several factors, including the horizontal orientation, which allows for more flexibility in configuring features both within the face and surrounding the face (e.g., arms) than the vertical orientation. Another important factor underlying *kaomoji* productivity is historical in nature. *kaomoji* were developed and popularized in Japan and other Asian countries whose scripts have always required multibyte character encodings, and whose users of electronic communication systems have significant experience working with characters beyond those found in the standard ASCII set.

Linguistic symbols from various scripts can be appropriated into the *kaomoji* for their resemblence to facial features, such as a winking eye, and authors of *kaomoji* sometimes use advanced Unicode techniques to decorate glyphs with elaborate combinations of diacritic marks. For example, the *kao-*

moji in the top righthand corner of Figure 1, includes an Arabic letter, and Thai vowel diacritics. Accurate detection of these tokens – and other common sequences of extra-linguistic symbol sequences – is important for normalization of social media text for downstream applications.

At the most basic level, the complex and unpredictable combinations of characters found within many *kaomoji* (often including punctuation and whitespace, as well as irregularly-used Unicode combining characters) can seriously confound sentence and word segmentation algorithms that attempt to operate on *kaomoji*-rich text; since segmentation is typically the first step in any text processing pipeline, issues here can cause a wide variety of problems downstream. Accurately removing or normalizing such sequences before attempting segmentation can ensure that existing NLP tools are able to effectively work with and analyze *kaomoji*-including text.

At a higher level, the inclusion of a particular *kaomoji* in a text represents a conscious decision on the part of the text's author, and fully interpreting the text necessarily involves a degree of interpretation of the *kaomoji* that they chose to include. European-style emoticons form a relatively closed set and are often fairly straightforward to interpret (both in terms of computational, as well as human, effort); *kaomoji*, on the other hand, are far more diverse, and interpretation is rarely simple.

In this paper, we present preliminary work on defining robust models for detecting kaomoji in social media text. Prior work on detecting and classifying these extra-linguistic sequences has relied on the presence of fixed attested patterns (see discussion in Section 2) for detection, and regular expressions for segmentation. While such approaches can capture the most common kaomoji and simple variants of them, the productive and creative nature of the phenomenon results in a non-negligible out-of-vocabulary problem. In this paper, we approach the problem by examining a broader class of possible sequences (see Section 4.2) for symmetry using a robust probabilistic context-free grammar with rule probabilities proportional to the symmetry or affinity of matched terminal items in the rule. Our PCFG is robust in the sense that every candidate sequence is guaranteed to have a valid parse. We use the resulting Viterbi best parse to provide a score to the candidate sequence – reranking our high recall list to achieve, via thresholds, high precision. In addition, we investigate unsupervised model adaptation, by incorporating Viterbi-best parses from a small set of attested *kaomoji* scraped from websites; and inducing grammars with a larger non-terminal set corresponding to regions of the face.

We present bootstrapping experiments for deriving highly functional, language independent models for detecting *kaomoji* in text, on multilingual Twitter data. Our approach can be used as part of a stand-alone detection model, or as input into semi-automatic *kaomoji* lexicon development. Before describing our approach, we will first present prior work on this class of emoticon.

2 Prior Work

Nakamura et al. (2003) presented a natural language dialogue system that learned a model for generating *kaomoji* face marks within Japanese chat. They trained a neural net to produce parts of the emoticon – mouth, eyes, arms and "optional things" as observed in real world data. They relied on a hand-constructed inventory of observed parts within each of the above classes, and stitched together predicted parts into a complete *kaomoji* using simple templates.

Tanaka et al. (2005) presented a finite-state chunking approach for detecting *kaomoji* in Japanese on-line bulletin boards using SVMs with simple features derived from a 7 character window. Training was performed on *kaomoji* dictionaries found online. They achieved precision and recall in the mid-80s on their test set, which was a significant recall improvement (17% absolute) and modest precision improvement (1.5%) over exact match within the dictionaries. They note certain kinds of errors, e.g., "(Thu)" which demonstrate that their chunking models are (unsurprisingly) not capturing the typical symmetry of *kaomoji*. In addition, they perform classification of the *kaomoji* into 6 rough categories (happy, sad, angry, etc.), achieving high performance (90% accuracy) using a string kernel within an SVM classifier.

Ptaszynski et al. (2010) present work on a large database of *kaomoji*, which makes use of an analysis of the gestures conveyed by the emoticons and their relation to a theory of non-verbal expressions. They created an extensive (approximately 10,000 entry) lexicon with 10 emotion classes, and used this database as the basis of both emoticon extraction from text and emotion classification. To detect an emoticon in text, their system (named 'CAO') looked for three symbols in a row from a vocabulary of the 455 most frequent symbols in their database. Their approach led to a 2.4% false negative rate when evaluated on 1,000 sentences extracted from Japanese blogs. Once detected, the system extracts the emoticon from the string using a gradual relaxation from exact match to approximate match, with various regular expressions depending on specific partial match criteria. A similar deterministic algorithm based on sequenced relaxation from exact match was used to assign affect to the emoticon.

Our work focuses on the emoticon detection stage, and differs from the above systems in a number of ways. First, while *kaomoji* were popularized in Asia, and are most prevalent in Asian languages, they not only found in messages in those languages. In Twitter, which is massively multilingual, we find *kaomoji* with some frequency in many languages, including European languages such as English and Portuguese, Semitic languages and a range of Asian languages. Our intent is to have a language independent algorithm that looks for such sequences in any message. Further, while we make use of online dictionaries as development data, we appreciate the productivity of the phenomenon and do not want to restrict the emoticons that we detect to those consisting of pre-observed characters. Hence we focus instead on characteristics of *kaomoji* that have been ignored in the above models: the frequent symmetry of the strings. We make use of context-free models, built in such a way as to guarantee a parse for any candidate sequence, which permits exploration of a much broader space of potential candidates than the prior approaches, using very general models and limited assumptions about the key components of the emoticons.

3 Data

Our starting resources consisted of a large, multilingual corpus of Twitter data as well as a smaller collection of *kaomoji* scraped from Internet sources. Our Twitter corpus consists of approximately 80 million messages collected using Twitter's "Streaming API" over a 50-day period from June through August 2011. The corpus is extremely linguistically diverse; human review of a small sample identified messages written in >30 languages. The messages themselves exhibit a wide variety of phenomena, including substantial use of different types of Internet slang and written dialect, as well as numerous forms of non-linguistic content such as emoticons and "ASCII art."

We took a two-pronged approach to developing a set of "gold-standard" *kaomoji*. Our first approach involved manually "scraping" real-world examples from the Internet. Using a series of handwritten scripts, we harvested 9,193 examples from several human-curated Internet websites devoted to collecting and exhibiting *kaomoji*. Many of these consisted of several discrete sub-units, typically including at least one "face" element along with a small amount of additional content. For example, consider the following *kaomoji*, which appeared in this exact form eight times in our Twitter corpus: ヾ(✿❛◡❛̤)ノぉはよぉ〜❤̤. Note that, in this case, the "face" is followed by a small amount of hiragana, and that the message concludes with a dingbat in the form of a "heart" symbol.[1]

Of these 9,193 scraped examples, we observed ≈3,700 to appear at least once in our corpus of Twitter messages, and ≈2,500 more than twice. The most common *kaomoji* occurred with frequencies in the low hundreds of thousands, although the frequency with which individual *kaomoji* appeared roughly followed a power-law distribution, meaning that there were a small number that occurred with great frequency and a much larger number that only appeared rarely.

From this scraped corpus, we attempted to identify a subset that consisted solely of "faces" to serve as a high-precision training set. After observing that nearly all of the faces involved a small number of characters bracketed one of a small set of natural grouping characters (parentheses, "curly braces,"

[1]Note as well that this *kaomoji* includes not only a wide variety of symbols, but that some of those symbols are themselves modified using combining diacritic marks. This is a common practice in modern *kaomoji*, and one that complicates analysis.

etc.), we extracted approximately 6,000 substrings matching a very simple regular expression pattern. This approach missed many *kaomoji*, and of the examples that it did detect, many were incomplete (in that they were missing any extra-bracketed content— arms, ears, whiskers, etc.) However, the contents of this "just faces" sub-corpus offered decent coverage of many of the core *kaomoji* phenomena in a relatively noise-free manner. As such, we found it to be useful as "seed" data for the grammar adaptation described in section 4.4.

In addition to our "scraped" *kaomoji* corpus, we constructed a smaller corpus of examples drawn directly from our Twitter corpus. The *kaomoji* phenomenon is complex enough that capturing it in its totality is difficult. However, it is possible to capture a subset of *kaomoji* by looking for regions of perfect lexical symmetry. This approach will capture many of the more regularly-formed and simple *kaomoji* (for example, ^ (−_−) ^), although it will miss many valid *kaomoji*. Using this approach, we identied 3,580 symmetrical candidate sequences; most of these were indeed *kaomoji*, although there were several false positives (for example, symmetrical sequences of repeated periods, question marks, etc.). Using simple regular expressions, we were able to remove 289 such false positives.

Interestingly, there was very little overlap between the corpus scraped from the Web and the symmetry corpus. A total of 39 *kaomoji* appeared in exactly the same form in both sets. We noted, however, that the *kaomoji* harvested from the Web tended to be longer and more elaborate than those identified from our Twitter corpus using the symmetry heuristic (Mann-Whitney U, $p < 0.001$), and as previously discussed, the Web *kaomoji* often contained one or more face elements. Thus we expanded our definition of overlap, and counted sequences from the symmetrical corpus that were substrings of scraped *kaomoji*. Using this criterion, we identified 177 possibly intersecting *kaomoji*. The fact that so few individual examples occurred in both corpora illustrates the extremely productive nature of the phenomenon.

4 Methods

4.1 Graphical similarity

The use of particular characters in *kaomoji* is ultimately based on their graphical appearance. For

0.9500	208d	fe5a	₍	﹚
0.9500	207d	fe5a	⁽	﹚
0.9500	1fef	2034	`	‴
0.9500	1fef	2033	`	″
0.9500	1fef	2032	`	′
0.9500	1489	1494	ᒉ	ᒔ
0.9500	055b	1fef	՛	`
0.9500	0500	13cf	Ԁ	Ꮟ
0.9500	0351	2e12	͑	⸒
0.9500	013f	14b2	Ŀ	ᒲ

Figure 2: Ten example character pairs with imperfect (but very high) symmetry identified by our algorithm. Columns are: score, hex code point 1, hex code point 2, glyph 1, glyph 2.

example, good face delimiters frequently include mated brackets or parentheses, since these elements naturally look as if they delimit material. Furthermore, there are many characters which are not technically "paired," but look roughly more-or-less symmetrical. For example, the Arabic-Indic digits ٩ and ۶ are commonly used as bracketing delimiters, for example: ٩◔̯◔۶. These characters can serve both as "arms" as well as "ears."

Besides bracketing, symmetry plays an additional role in *kaomoji* construction. Glyphs that make good "eyes" are often round; "noses" are often symmetric about their central axis. Therefore a measure of graphical similarity between characters is desirable.

To that end, we developed a very simple measure of similarity. From online sources, we downloaded a sample glyph for each code point in the Unicode Basic Multilingual Plane, and extracted a bitmap for each. In comparing two glyphs we first scale them to have the same aspect ratio if necessary, and we then compute the proportion of shared pixels between them, with a perfect match being 1 and the worst match being 0. We can thus compute whether two glyphs look similar; whether one glyph is a good mirror image of the other (by comparing glyph A with the mirror image of glyph B); and whether a glyph is (vertically) symmetric (by computing the similarity of the glyph and its vertical mirror image).

The method, while clearly simple-minded, nonetheless produces plausible results, as seen in Figure 2, which shows the best 10 candidates for mirror image character pairs. We also calculate the same score without flipping the image vertically, which is also used to score possible symbol matches, as detailed in Section 4.3.

4.2 Candidate extraction

We perform candidate *kaomoji* extraction via a very simple hidden Markov model, which segments all strings of Unicode graphemes into contiguous regions that are either primarily linguistic (mainly language encoding symbols[2]) or primarily non-linguistic (mainly punctuation, or other symbols). Our candidate emoticons, then, are this extensive list of mainly non-linguistic symbol sequences. This is a high recall approach, returning most sequences that contain valid emoticons, but quite low precision, since it includes many other sequences as well (extended runs of punctuation, etc.).

The simple HMM consists of 2 states: call them A (mainly linguistic) and @ (mainly non-linguistic). Since there are two emitted symbol classes (linguistic L and non-linguistic N), each HMM state must have two emission probabilities, one for its dominant symbol class (L in A and N in @) and one for the other symbol class. Non-linguistic symbols occur quite often in linguistic sequences, as punctuation for example. However, sequences of, say, 3 or more in a row are not particularly frequent. Similarly, linguistic symbols occur often in *kaomoji*, though not often in sequences of, say, 3 or more. Hence, to segment into contiguous sequences of a certain number in a row, the probability of transition from state A to state @ or vice versa must be significantly lower than the probability of emitting one or two N from A states or L from @ states. We thus have an 8 parameter HMM (four transition and four emission probabilities) that was coarsely parameterized to have the above properties, and used it to extract candidate non-linguistic sequences for evaluation by our PCFG model.

Note that this approach does have the limitation that it will trim off some linguistic symbols that occur on the periphery of an emoticon. Future versions of this part of the system will address this issue by extending the HMM. For this paper, we made use of a slightly modified version of this simple HMM for candidate extraction. The modifications involved the addition of a special input state for whitespace and full-stop punctuation, which helped prevent certain very common classes of false-positive.

[2]Defined as a character having the Unicode "letter" character property.

rule	score	rule	score
$X \rightarrow a\, X\, b$	S(a,b)	$X \rightarrow a\, b$	S(a,b)
$X \rightarrow a\, X$	ϵ	$X \rightarrow X\, a$	ϵ
$X \rightarrow a$	δ	$X \rightarrow X\, X$	γ

Table 1: Rule schemata for producing PCFG

4.3 Baseline grammar induction

We perform a separate PCFG induction for every candidate emoticon sequence, based on a small set of rule templates methods for assigning rule weights. By inducing small, example-specific PCFGs, we ensure that every example has a valid parse, without growing the grammar to the point that the grammar constant would seriously impact parser efficiency.

Table 1 shows the rule schemata that we used for this paper. The resulting PCFG would have a single non-terminal (X) and the variables a and b would be instantiated with terminal items taken from the candidate sequence. Each instantiated rule receives a probability proportional to the assigned score. For the rules that "pair" symbols a and b, a score is assigned in two ways, call them $S_1(a, b)$ and $S_2(a, b)$ (they will be defined in a moment). Then $S(a, b) = \max(S_1(a, b)$ and $S_2(a, b))$. If $S(a, b) < \theta$, for some threshold θ,[3] then no rule is generated. S_1 is the graphical similarity of the first symbol with the vertical mirror image of the second symbol, calculated as presented in Section 4.1. This will give a high score for things like balanced parentheses. S_2 is the graphical similarity of the first symbol with the second symbol (not vertically flipped), which gives high scores to the same or similar symbols. This permits matches for, say, eyes that are not symmetric due to an orientation of the face, e.g., (ˀثˀ). The other parameters (ϵ, δ and γ) are included to allow for, but penalize, unmatched symbols in the sequence.

All possible rules for a given sequence are instantiated using these templates, by placing each symbol in the a slot with all subsequent symbols in the b slot and scoring, as well as creating all rules with just a alone for that symbol. For example, if we are given the *kaomoji* (○_○;) specific rules would be created if the similarity scores were above threshold. For the second symbol '○', the algorithm would evaluate the

[3]For this paper, θ was chosen to be 0.7.

similarity between 'o' and each of the four symbols to its right _, o, ; and).

The resulting PCFG is normalized by summing the score for each rule and normalizing by the score. The grammar is then transformed to a weakly equivalent CNF by binarizing the ternary rules and introducing preterminal non-terminals. This grammar is then provided to the parser[4], which returns the Viterbi best parse of the candidate emoticon along with its probability. The score is then converted to an approximate perplexity by dividing the negative log probability by the number of unique symbols in the sequence and taking the exponential.

4.4 Grammar enhancement and adaptation

The baseline grammar induction approach outlined in the previous section can be improved in a couple of ways, without sacrificing the robustness of the approach. One way is through grammar adaptation based on automatic parses of attested *kaomoji*. The other is by increasing the number of non-terminals in the grammar, according to a prior understanding of their typical (canonical) structure. We shall discuss each in turn.

Given a small corpus of attested emoticons (in our case, the "just faces" sub-corpus described in section 3), we can apply the parser above to those examples, and extract the Viterbi best parses into an automatically created treebank. From that treebank, we extract counts of rule productions and use these rule counts to inform our grammar estimation. The benefit of this approach is that we will obtain additional probability mass for frequently observed constructions in that corpus, thus preferring commonly associated pairs within the grammar. Of course, the corpus only has a small fraction of the possible symbols that we hope to cover in our robust approach, so we want to incorporate this information in a way that does not limit the kinds of sequences we can parse.

We can accomplish this by using simple Maximum a Posteriori (MAP) adaptation of the grammar (Bacchiani et al., 2006). In this scenario, we will first use our baseline method of grammar induction, using the schemata shown in Table 1. The scores derived in that process then serve as prior counts for the rules in the grammar, ensuring that all of these rules continue to receive probability mass. We then add in the counts for each of the rules from the treebank. Many of the rules may have been unobserved in the corpus, in which case they receive no additional counts; observed rules, however, will receive extra weight proportional to their frequency in that corpus. Note that these additional weights can be scaled according to a given parameter. After incorporating these additional counts, the grammar is normalized and parsing is performed as before. Of course, this process can be iterated – a new automatic treebank can be produced based on an adapted grammar, and so on.

In addition to grammar adaptation, we can enrich our grammars by increasing the non-terminal sets. To do this, we created a nested hierarchy of "regions" of the emoticons, with constraints related to the canonical composition of the faces, e.g., eyes are inside of faces, noses/mouths between eyes, etc. These non-terminals replace our generic non-terminal X in the rule schemata. For the current paper, we included the following five "region" non-terminals: *ITEM, OUT, FACE, EYES, NM*. The non-terminal *ITEM* is intended as a top-most non-terminal to allow multiple emoticons in a single sequence, via an *ITEM* $\rightarrow$ *ITEM ITEM* production. None of the others non-terminals have repeating productions of that sort – so this replaces the X $\rightarrow$ X X production from Table 1.

Every production (other than *ITEM* $\rightarrow$ *ITEM ITEM*) has zero or one non-terminals on the right-hand side. In our new schemata, non-terminals on the left-hand side can only have non-terminals on the right-hand side at the same or lower levels. This enforces the nesting constraint, i.e., that eyes are inside of the face. Levels can be omitted however – e.g., eyes but no explicit face delimiter – hence we can "skip" a level using unary projections, e.g., FACE $\rightarrow$ EYES. Those will come with a "skip level" weight. Categories can also rewrite to the same level (with a "stay level" weight) or rewrite to the next level after emitting symbols (with a "move to next level" weight).

To encode a preference to move to the next level rather than to stay at the same level, we assign a weight of 1 to moving to the next level and a weight of 0.5 to staying at the same level. The "skip"

[4]We used the BUBS parser (Bodenstab et al., 2011). `http://code.google.com/p/bubs-parser/`

rule			score
ITEM	→	*ITEM ITEM*	γ
ITEM	→	*OUT*	γ
OUT	→	*a OUT b*	S(*a*,*b*) + 0.5
OUT	→	*a OUT*	ϵ + 0.5
OUT	→	*OUT a*	ϵ + 0.5
OUT	→	*a FACE b*	S(*a*,*b*) + 1
OUT	→	*a FACE*	ϵ +1
OUT	→	*FACE a*	ϵ +1
OUT	→	*FACE*	0.5
FACE	→	*a FACE b*	S(*a*,*b*) + 0.5
FACE	→	*a FACE*	ϵ + 0.5
FACE	→	*FACE a*	ϵ + 0.5
FACE	→	*a EYES b*	S(*a*,*b*) + 1
FACE	→	*a EYES*	ϵ +1
FACE	→	*EYES a*	ϵ +1
FACE	→	*EYES*	0.1
EYES	→	*a EYES b*	S(*a*,*b*) + 0.5
EYES	→	*a EYES*	ϵ + 0.5
EYES	→	*EYES a*	ϵ + 0.5
EYES	→	*a NM b*	S(*a*,*b*) + 1
EYES	→	*a NM*	ϵ +1
EYES	→	*NM a*	ϵ +1
EYES	→	*NM*	0.1
EYES	→	*a b*	S(*a*,*b*) + 1
NM	→	*a NM*	ϵ
NM	→	*NM a*	ϵ
NM	→	*a*	δ

Table 2: Rule schemata for expanded non-terminal set

weights depend on the level, e.g., skipping OUT should be cheap (weight of 0.5), while skipping the others more expensive (weight of 0.1). These weights are like counts, and are added to the similarity counts when deriving the probability of the rule. Finally, there is a rule in the schemata in Table 1 with a pair of symbols and no middle non-terminal. This is most appropriate for eyes, hence will only be generated at that level. Similarly, the single symbol on the right-hand side is for the NM (nose/mouth) region. Table 2 presents our expanded rule schemata.

Note that the grammar generated with this expanded set of non-terminals is robust, just as the earlier grammar is, in that every sequence is guaranteed to have a parse. Further, it can be adapted using the same methods presented earlier in this section.

5 Experimental Results

Using the candidate extraction methodology described in section 4.2, we extracted 1.6 million distinct candidates from our corpus of 80 million Twitter messages (candidates often appeared in multiple messages). These candidates included genuine emoticons, as well as extended strings of punctuation and other "noisy" chunks of text. Genuine *kaomoji* were often picked up with some amount of leading or trailing punctuation, for example: "·.\(´▽`)/"; other times, *kaomoji* beginning with linguistic characters were truncated: (^。*)ʃ.

We provided these candidates to our parser under four different conditions, each one producing 1.5 million parse trees: the single non-terminal approach described in section 4.3 or the enhanced multiple non-terminal approach described in section 4.4, both with and without training via the Maximum A Posteriori approach described in section 4.4.

Using the weighted-inside-score method described in section 4.3, we produced a ranked list of candidate emoticons from each condition's output. "Well-scoring" candidates were ones for which the parser was able to construct a low-cost parse. We evaluated our approach in two ways. The first way examined precision— how many of the best-scoring candidate sequences actually contained *kaomoji*? Manually reviewing all 1.6 million candidates was not feasible, so we evaluated this aspect of our system's performance on a small subset of its output. Computational considerations forced us to process our large corpus in parallel, meaning that our set of 1.6 million candidate *kaomoji* was already partitioned into 160 sets of ≈10,000 candidates each. We manually reviewed the top 1,000 sorted results from one of these partitions, and flagged any entries that did not contain or consist of a face-like *kaomoji*. The results of each condition are presented in table 3.

The second evaluation approach we will examine looks at how our method compares with the trigram-based approach described by (Yamada et al., 2007) (as described by (Ptaszynski et al., 2010)). We trained both smoothed and unsmoothed language models [5] on the "just faces" sub-corpus used for the A Posteriori grammar enhancement, and computed perplexity measurements for the same set ≈10,000 candidates used previously. Table 3 presents these results; clearly, a smoothed trigram model can achieve good results. The unsmoothed model at first glance seems to have performed very well; note, however, that only approximately 600 (out of nearly 10,000) candidates were "matched" by the unsmoothed model (i.e., they did not contain any OOV symbols and therefore had finite perplexity scores), yielding a very small but high-precision set of emoticons.

Looking at precision, the model-based approaches outperformed our grammar approach. It

[5]Using the OpenGrm ngram language modeling toolkit.

Condition	P@1000	MAP
Single Nonterm, Untrained	0.662	0.605
Single Nonterm, Trained	0.80	0.945
Multiple Nonterm, Untrained	0.795	0.932
Multiple Nonterm, Trained	0.885	0.875
Unsmoothed 3-gram	0.888	0.985
Smoothed 3-gram	0.905	0.956
Mixed, Single Nonterm, Untrained	0.662	0.902
Mixed, Single Nonterm, Trained	0.804	0.984
Mixed, Multiple Nonterm, Untrained	0.789	0.932
Mixed, Multiple Nonterm, Trained	0.878	0.977

Table 3: Experimental Results.

should be noted, however, that the trigram approach was much less tolerant of certain non-standard formulations involving novel characters or irregular formulations ((˘⌣˘) and ／(ˆoˆ)＼ are examples of *kaomoji* that our grammar-based approach ranked more highly than did the trigram approach). The two approaches also had different failure profiles. The grammar approach's false positives tended to be symmetrical sequences of punctuation, whereas the language models' were more variable. Were we to review a larger selection of candidates, we believe that the structure-capturing nature of the grammar approach would enable it to outperform the more simplistic approach.

We also attempted a hybrid "mixed" approach in which we used the language models to re-rank the top 1,000 "best" candidates from our parser's output. This generally resulted in improved performance, and for some conditions the improvement was substantial. Future work will explore this approach in greater detail and over larger amounts of data.

6 Discussion

We describe an almost entirely unsupervised approach to detecting *kaomoji* in irregular, real-world text. In its baseline state, our system is able to accurately identify a large number of examples using a very simple set of templates, and can distinguish *kaomoji* from other non-linguistic content (punctuation, etc.). Using minimal supervision, we were able to effect a dramatic increase in our system's performance. Visual comparison of the "untrained" results with the "trained" results was instructive. The untrained systems' results were very heavily influenced by their template rules' strong preference for visual symmetry. Many instances of symmetrical punctuation sequences (e.g., `..?..`) ended up being ranked more highly than even fairly simple *kaomoji*, and in the absence of other information, the length of the input strings also played a too-important role in their rankings.

The MAP-ehanced systems' results, on the other hand, retained their strong preference for symmetry, but were also influenced by the patterns and characters present in their training data. For example, two of the top-ranked "false positives" from the enhanced system were the sequences `>,<` and `= =`, both of which (while symmetrical) also contain characters often seen in *kaomoji*. By using more structurally diverse training data, we expect further improvements in this area. Also, our system currently relies on a very small number of relatively simplistic grammar templates; expanding these to encode additional structure may also help.

Due to our current scoring mechanism, our parser is biased against certain categories of *kaomoji*. Particularly poorly-scored are complex creations such as (((I̅•I̅≡I̅•I))). In this example, the large number of combining characters and lack of obvious nesting therein confounded our templates and produced expensive parse trees. Future work will involve improved handling of such cases, either by modified parsing schemes or additional templates.

One other area of future work is to match particular *kaomoji*, or fragments of *kaomoji* (e.g. particular eyes), to particular affective states, or other features of the text. Some motifs are already well known: for example, there is wide use of `TT`, or the similar-looking Korean *hangeul* vowel *yu*, to represent crying eyes. We propose to do this initially by computing the association between particular *kaomoji* and words in the text. Such associations may yield more than just information on the likely affect associated with a *kaomoji*. So, for example, using pointwise mutual information as a measure of association, we found that in our Twitter corpus, (*^_^*) seems to be highly associated with tweets about Korean pop music, *−* with Brazilian postings, and °\(^▽^)/° with Indonesian postings. Such associations presumably reflect cultural preferences, and could prove useful in identifying the provenance of a message even if more conventional linguistic techniques fail.

References

Michiel Bacchiani, Michael Riley, Brian Roark, and Richard Sproat. 2006. MAP adaptation of stochastic grammars. *Computer Speech and Language*, 20(1):41–68.

Nathan Bodenstab, Aaron Dunlop, Keith Hall, and Brian Roark. 2011. Adaptive beam-width prediction for efficient cyk parsing. In *Proceedings of the 49th Annual Meeting of the Association for Computational Linguistics*, pages 440–449.

Junpei Nakamura, Takeshi Ikeda, Nobuo Inui, and Yoshiyuki Kotani. 2003. Learning face mark for natural language dialogue system. In *Proc. Conf. IEEE Int'l Conf. Natural Language Processing and Knowledge Eng*, pages 180–185.

Michal Ptaszynski, Jacek Maciejewski, Pawel Dybala, Rafal Rzepka, and Kenji Araki. 2010. Cao: A fully automatic emoticon analysis system based on theory of kinesics. *IEEE Transactions on Affective Computing*, 1:46–59.

Yuki Tanaka, Hiroya Takamura, and Manabu Okumura. 2005. Extraction and classification of facemarks with kernel methods. In *Proc. 10th Int'l Conf. Intelligent User Interfaces*.

T. Yamada, S. Tsuchiya, S. Kuroiwa, and F. Ren. 2007. Classification of facemarks using n-gram. In *International Conference on Natural Language Processing and Knowledge Engineering*, pages 322–327.

Language Identification for Creating Language-Specific Twitter Collections

Shane Bergsma[†] **Paul McNamee**[†,♮] **Mossaab Bagdouri**[⋆] **Clayton Fink**[♮] **Theresa Wilson**[†]
[†]Human Language Technology Center of Excellence, Johns Hopkins University
[♮]Johns Hopkins University Applied Physics Laboratory, Laurel, MD
[⋆]Department of Computer Science, University of Maryland, College Park, MD
sbergsma@jhu.edu, mcnamee@jhu.edu, mossaab@umd.edu, clayton.fink@jhuapl.edu, taw@jhu.edu

Abstract

Social media services such as Twitter offer an immense volume of real-world linguistic data. We explore the use of Twitter to obtain authentic user-generated text in low-resource languages such as Nepali, Urdu, and Ukrainian. Automatic language identification (LID) can be used to extract language-specific data from Twitter, but it is unclear how well LID performs on short, informal texts in low-resource languages. We address this question by annotating and releasing a large collection of tweets in nine languages, focusing on confusable languages using the Cyrillic, Arabic, and Devanagari scripts. This is the first publicly-available collection of LID-annotated tweets in non-Latin scripts, and should become a standard evaluation set for LID systems. We also advance the state-of-the-art by evaluating new, highly-accurate LID systems, trained both on our new corpus and on standard materials only. Both types of systems achieve a huge performance improvement over the existing state-of-the-art, correctly classifying around 98% of our gold standard tweets. We provide a detailed analysis showing how the accuracy of our systems vary along certain dimensions, such as the tweet-length and the amount of in- and out-of-domain training data.

1 Introduction

Twitter is an online social-networking service that lets users send and receive short texts called *tweets*. Twitter is enormously popular; more than 50 million users log in daily and billions of tweets are sent each month.[1] Tweets are publicly-available by default and thus provide an enormous and growing free resource of authentic, unedited text by ordinary people. Researchers have used Twitter to study how human language varies by time zone (Kiciman, 2010), census area (Eisenstein et al., 2011), gender (Burger et al., 2011), and ethnicity (Fink et al., 2012). Twitter also provides a wealth of user dialog, and a variety of dialog acts have been observed (Ritter et al., 2010) and predicted (Ritter et al., 2011).

Of course, working with Twitter is not all roses and rainbows. Twitter is a difficult domain because unlike, for example, news articles, tweets are short (limited to 140 characters), vary widely in style, and contain many spelling and grammatical errors. Moreover, unlike articles written by a particular news organization, a corpus constructed from Twitter will contain tweets in many different languages.

This latter point is particularly troubling because the majority of language-processing technology is predicated on knowing which language is being processed. We are pursuing a long-term effort to build social media collections in a variety of low-resource languages, and we need robust language identification (LID) technology. While LID is often viewed as a solved problem (McNamee, 2005), recent research has shown that LID can be made arbitrarily difficult by choosing domains with (a) informal writing, (b) lots of languages to choose from, (c) very short texts, and (d) unbalanced data (Hughes et al., 2006; Baldwin and Lui, 2010). Twitter exhibits all of these properties. While the problem of LID on Twitter has been considered previously (Tromp and Pechenizkiy, 2011; Carter et al., 2013), these studies have only targeted five or six western European languages, and not the diversity of languages and writing systems that we would like to process.

[1] http://mashable.com/2011/09/08/Twitter-has-100-million-active-users/

Our main contribution is the release of a large collection of tweets in nine languages using the Cyrillic, Arabic, and Devanagari alphabets. We test different methods for obtaining tweets in a given target language (§2). We then use an online crowdsourcing platform to have these tweets annotated by fluent speakers of that language (§3). We generate over 18,000 triple-consensus tweets, providing the first publicly-available collection of LID-annotated tweets in non-Latin scripts. The annotated corpus is available online at: `http://apl.jhu.edu/~paulmac/lid.html`. We anticipate our multilingual Twitter collection becoming a standard evaluation set for LID systems.

We also implement two LID approaches and evaluate these approaches against state-of-the-art competitors. §4.1 describes a discriminative classifier that leverages both the tweet text and the tweet metadata (such as the user name, location, and landing pages for shortened URLs). §4.2 describes an efficient tool based on compression language models. Both types of systems achieve a huge improvement over existing state-of-the-art approaches, including the Google Compact Language Detector (part of the Chrome browser), and a recent LID system from Lui and Baldwin (2011). Finally, we provide further analysis of our systems in this unique domain, showing how accuracy varies with the tweet-length and the amount of in-domain and out-of-domain training data. In addition to the datasets, we are releasing our compression language model tool for public use.

2 Acquiring Language-Specific Tweets

We use two strategies to collect tweets in specific languages: (§2.1) we collect tweets by users who follow language-specific Twitter sources, and (§2.2) we use the Twitter API to collect tweets from users who are likely to speak the target language.

2.1 Followers of Language-Specific *Sources*

Our first method is called the *Sources* method and involves a three-stage process. First, Twitter *sources* for the target language are manually identified. Sources are Twitter users or feeds who: (a) tweet in the target language, (b) have a large number of followers, and (c) act as hubs (i.e., have a high followers-to-following ratio). Twitter sources are typically news or media outlets (e.g. BBC News), celebrities, politicians, governmental organizations, but they may just be prominent bloggers or tweeters.

Once sources are identified, we use the Twitter API (`dev.twitter.com`) to query each source for its list of *followers*. We then query the user data for the followers in batches of 100 tweets. For users whose data is public, a wealth of information is returned, including the total number of tweets and their most recent tweet. For users who had tweeted above a minimum number of times. and whose most-recent-tweet tweet was in the character set for the target language, we obtained their most recent 100-200 tweets and added them to our collection.[2]

While we have used the above approach to acquire data in a number of different languages, for the purposes of our annotated corpus (§3), we select the subsets of users who exclusively follow sources in one of our nine target languages (Table 1). We also filter tweets that do not contain at least one character in the target's corresponding writing system (we plan to address *romanized* tweets in future work).

2.2 Direct Twitter-API Collection

While we are most interested in users who follow news articles, we also tested other methods for obtaining language-specific tweets. First, we used the Twitter API to collect tweets from locations where we expected to get some number of tweets in the target language. We call this method the *Twit-API* collection method. To geolocate our tweets, the Twitter API's geotag method allowed us to collect tweets within a specified radius of a given set of coordinates in latitude and longitude. To gather a sample of tweets in our target languages, we queried for tweets from cities with populations of at least 200,000 where speakers of the target language are prominent (e.g., Karachi, Pakistan for Urdu; Tehran, Iran for Farsi; etc.). We collected tweets within a radius of 25 miles of the geocoordinates. We also used the Search API to persistently poll for tweets from users identified by Twitter as being in the queried location. For Urdu, we also relied on the language-

[2] Tromp and Pechenizkiy (2011) also manually identified language-specific Twitter feeds, but they use tweets from these sources directly as gold standard data, while we target the users who simply follow such sources. We expect our approach to obtain more-authentic and less-edited user language.

identification code returned by the API for each tweet; we filter all our geolocated Urdu tweets that are not marked as Urdu.

We also obtained tweets through an information-retrieval approach that has been used elsewhere for creating minority language corpora (Ghani et al., 2001). We computed the 25 most frequent *unique* words in a number of different languages (that is, words that do not occur in the vocabularies of other languages). Unfortunately, we found no way to *enforce* that the Twitter API return only tweets containing one or more of our search terms (e.g., returned tweets for Urdu were often in Arabic and did not contain our Urdu search terms). There is a lack of documentation on what characters are supported by the search API; it could be that the API cannot handle certain of our terms. We thus leave further investigation of this method for future work.

3 Annotating Tweets by Language

The general LID task is to take as input some piece of text, and to produce as output a prediction of what language the text is written in. Our annotation and prediction systems operate at the level of individual tweets. An alternative would have been to assume that each user only tweets in a single language, and to make predictions on an aggregation of multiple tweets. We operate on individual tweets mainly because (A) we would like to quantify how often users switch between languages and (B) we are also interested in domains and cases where only tweet-sized amounts of text are available. When we do have multiple tweets per user, we can always aggregate the scores on individual predictions (§6 has some experimental results using prediction aggregation).

Our human annotation therefore also focuses on validating the language of individual tweets. Tweets verified by three independent annotators are accepted into our final gold-standard data.

3.1 Amazon Mechanical Turk

To access annotators with fluency in each language, we crowdsourced the annotation using Amazon Mechanical Turk (`mturk.com`). AMT is an online labor marketplace that allows *requesters* to post tasks for completion by paid human *workers*. Crowdsourcing via AMT has been shown to provide high-quality data for a variety of NLP tasks (Snow et al., 2008; Callison-Burch and Dredze, 2010), including multilingual annotation efforts in translation (Zaidan and Callison-Burch, 2011b), dialect identification (Zaidan and Callison-Burch, 2011a), and building bilingual lexicons (Irvine and Klementiev, 2010).

3.2 Annotation Task

From the tweets obtained in §2, we took a random sample in each target language, and posted these tweets for annotation on AMT. Each tweet in the sample was assigned to a particular AMT job; each job comprised the annotation of 20 tweets. The job description requested workers that are fluent in the target language and gave an example of valid and invalid tweets in that language. The job instructions asked workers to mark whether each tweet was written for speakers of the target language. If the tweet combines multiple languages, workers were asked to mark as the target language if "most of the text is in [that language] excluding URLs, hash-tags, etc." Jobs were presented to workers as HTML pages with three buttons alongside each tweet for validating the language. For example, for Nepali, a Worker can mark that a tweet is 'Nepali', 'Not Nepali', or 'Not sure.' We paid $0.05 per job and requested that each job be completed by three workers.

3.3 Quality Control

To ensure high annotation quality, we follow our established practices in only allowing our tasks to be completed by workers who have previously completed at least 50 jobs on AMT, and who have had at least 85% of their jobs approved. Our jobs also display each tweet as an image; this prevents workers from pasting the tweet into existing online language processing services (like Google Translate).

We also have *control* tweets in each job to allow us to evaluate worker performance. A *positive* control is a tweet known to be in the target language; a *negative* control is a tweet known to be in a different language. Between three to six of the twenty tweets in each job were controls. The controls are taken from the sources used in our *Sources* method (§2.1); e.g., our Urdu controls come from sources like BBC Urdu's Twitter feed. To further validate the controls, we also applied our open-domain LID system (§4.2) and filtered any Source tweets whose

Language	Method	Purity	Gold Tweets
Arabic	*Sources*	100%	1174
Farsi	*Sources*	100%	2512
Urdu	*Sources*	**55.4%**	1076
Arabic	*Twit-API*	99.9%	1254
Farsi	*Twit-API*	99.7%	2366
Urdu	*Twit-API*	**61.0%**	1313
Hindi	*Sources*	97.5%	1214
Nepali	*Sources*	97.3%	1681
Marathi	*Sources*	91.4%	1157
Russian	*Sources*	99.8%	2005
Bulgarian	*Sources*	92.2%	1886
Ukrainian	*Sources*	**14.3%**	631

Table 1: Statistics of the Annotated Multilingual Twitter Corpus: 18,269 total tweets in nine languages.

predicted language was not the expected language. Our negative controls are validated tweets in a language that uses the same alphabet as the target (e.g., our negative controls for Ukrainian were taken from our LID-validated Russian and Bulgarian sources).

We collect aggregate statistics for each Worker over the control tweets of all their completed jobs. We conservatively discard any annotations by workers who get below 80% accuracy on either the positive or negative control tweets.

3.4 Dataset Statistics

Table 1 gives the number of triple-validated 'Gold' tweets in each language, grouped into those using the Arabic, Devanagari and Cyrillic writing systems. The Arabic data is further divided into tweets acquired using the *Sources* and *Twit-API* methods. Table 1 also gives the *Purity* of the acquired results; that is, the percentage of acquired tweets that were indeed in the target language. The *Purity* is calculated as the number of triple-verified gold tweets divided by the total number of tweets where the three annotators agreed in the annotation (thus triply-marked either Yes, No, or Not sure).

For major languages (e.g. Arabic and Russian), we can accurately obtain tweets in the target language, perhaps obviating the need for LID. For the Urdu sets, however, a large percentage of tweets are not in Urdu, and thus neither collection method is reliable. An LID tool is needed to validate the data. A native Arabic speaker verified that most of our invalid Urdu tweets were Arabic. Ukrainian is the most glaringly impure language that we collected, with less than 15% of our intended tweets actually in Ukrainian. Russian is widely spoken in Ukraine and seems to be the dominant language on Twitter, but more analysis is required. Finally, Marathi and Bulgarian also have significant impurities.

The complete annotation of all nine languages cost only around $350 USD. While not insignificant, this was a small expense relative to the total human effort we are expending on this project. Scaling our approach to hundreds of languages would only cost on the order of a few thousand dollars, and we are investigating whether such an effort could be supported by enough fluent AMT workers.

4 Language Identification Systems

We now describe the systems we implemented and/or tested on our annotated data. All the approaches are *supervised* learners, trained from a collection of language-annotated texts. At test time, the systems choose an output language based on the information they have derived from the annotated data.

4.1 *LogR*: Discriminative LID

We first adopt a discriminative approach to LID. Each tweet to be classified has its relevant information encoded in a feature vector, $\bar{x}$. The annotated training data can be represented as N pairs of labels and feature vectors: $\{(y^1, \bar{x}^1), ..., (y^N, \bar{x}^N)\}$. To train our model, we use (regularized) logistic regression (a.k.a. maximum entropy) since it has been shown to perform well on a range of NLP tasks and its probabilistic outputs are useful for downstream processing (such as aggregating predictions over multiple tweets). In multi-class logistic regression, the probability of each class takes the form of exponential functions over features:

$$p(y = k|\bar{x}) = \frac{\exp(\bar{w}_k \cdot \bar{x})}{\sum_j \exp(\bar{w}_j \cdot \bar{x})}$$

For LID, the classifier predicts the language k that has the highest probability (this is also the class with highest weighted combination of features, $\bar{w}_k \cdot \bar{x}$). The training procedure tunes the weights to optimize for correct predictions on training data, subject to a tunable L2-regularization penalty on the weight vector norm. For our experiments, we train and test our logistic regression classifier (*LogR*) using the efficient LIBLINEAR package (Fan et al., 2008).

We use two types of features in our classifier:

Character Features encode the character N-grams in the input text; characters are the standard information source for most LID systems (Cavnar and Trenkle, 1994; Baldwin and Lui, 2010). We have a unique feature for each unique N-gram in our training data. N-grams of up-to-four characters were optimal on development data. Each feature value is the (smoothed) log-count of how often the corresponding N-gram occurs in that instance. Prior to extracting the N-grams, we preprocess each tweet to remove URLs, hash-tags, user mentions, punctuation and we normalize all digits to 0.

Meta features encode user-provided information beyond the tweet text. Similar information has previously been used to improve the accuracy of LID classifiers on European-language tweets (Carter et al., 2013). We have features for the tokens in the Twitter user name, the screen name, and self-reported user location. We also have features for prefixes of these tokens, and flags for whether the name and location are in the Latin script. Our meta features also include features for the hash-tags, user-mentions, and URLs in the tweet. We provide features for the protocol (e.g. http), hostname, and top-level domain (e.g. `.com`) of each link in a tweet. For shortened URLs (e.g. via `bit.ly`), we query the URL server to obtain the final link destination, and provide the URL features for this destination link.

4.2 *PPM*: Compression-Based LID

Our next tool uses compression language models, which have been proposed for a variety of NLP tasks including authorship attribution (Pavelec et al., 2009), text classification (Teahan, 2000; Frank et al., 2000), spam filtering (Bratko et al., 2006), and LID (Benedetto et al., 2002). Our method is based on the prediction by partial matching (PPM) family of algorithms and we use the PPM-A variant (Cleary et al., 1984). The algorithm processes a string and determines the number of bits required to encode each character using a variable-length context. It requires only a single parameter, the maximal order, n; we use $n = 5$ for the experiments in this paper. Given training data for a number of languages, the method seeks to minimize cross-entropy and thus selects the language which would most compactly encode the text we are attempting to classify.

Language	Wikip.	All
Arabic	372 MB	1058 MB
Farsi	229 MB	798 MB
Urdu	30 MB	50 MB
Hindi	235 MB	518 MB
Nepali	31 MB	31 MB
Marathi	32 MB	66 MB
Russian	563 MB	564 MB
Bulgarian	301 MB	518 MB
Ukrainian	461 MB	463 MB

Table 2: Size of other *PPM* training materials.

We train this method both on our Twitter data and on large collections of other material. These materials include corpora obtained from news sources, Wikipedia, and government bodies. For our experiments we divide these materials into two sets: (1) just Wikipedia and (2) all sources, including Wikipedia. Table 2 gives the sizes of these sets.

4.3 Comparison Systems

We compare our two new systems with the best-available commercial and academic software.

TextCat: TextCat[3] is a widely-used stand-alone LID program. Is is an implementation of the N-gram-based algorithm of Cavnar and Trenkle (1994), and supports identification in "about 69 languages" in its downloadable form. Unfortunately, the available models do not support all of our target languages, nor are they compatible with the standard UTF-8 Unicode character encoding. We therefore modified the code to process UTF-8 characters and re-trained the system on our Twitter data (§5).

Google CLD: Google's Chrome browser includes a tool for language-detection (the Google *Compact Language Detector*), and this tool is included as a library within Chrome's open-source code. Mike McCandless ported this library to its own open source project.[4] The CLD tool makes predictions using text 4-grams. It is designed for detecting the language of web pages, and can take meta-data hints from the domain of the webpage and/or the declared webpage

[3] `http://odur.let.rug.nl/vannoord/TextCat/`

[4] `http://code.google.com/p/chromium-compact-language-detector/`

Dataset	Train	Development	Test
Arabic	2254	1171	1191
Devanagari	2099	991	962
Cyrillic	2243	1133	1146

Table 3: Number of tweets used in experiments, by writing system/classification task

encoding, but it also works on stand-alone text.[5] We use it in its original, unmodified form. While there are few details in the source code itself, the training data for this approach was apparently obtained through Google's internal data collections.

***Lui and Baldwin '11*:** Lui and Baldwin (2011) recently released a stand-alone LID tool, which they call `langid.py`.[6] They compared this system to state-of-the-art LID methods and found it "to be faster whilst maintaining competitive accuracy." We use this system with its provided models only, as the software `readme` notes "training a model for langid.py is a non-trivial process, due to the large amount of computations required." The sources of the provided models are described in Lui and Baldwin (2011). Although many languages are supported, we restrict the system to only choose between our data's target languages (§5).

5 Experiments

The nine languages in our annotated data use one of three different writing systems: Arabic, Devanagari, or Cyrillic. We therefore define three classification tasks, each choosing between three languages that have the same writing system. We divide our annotated corpus into training, development and test data for these experiments (Table 3). For the Arabic data, we merge the tweets obtained via our two collection methods (§2); for Devanagari/Cyrillic, all tweets are obtained using the *Sources* method. We ensure that tweets by a unique Twitter *user* occur in at most *only one* of the sets. The proportion of each language in each set is roughly the same as the proportions of gold tweets in Table 1. All of our Twitter-trained systems learn their models from this training data, while all hyperparameter tuning (such as tuning the regularization parameter of the *LogR* classifier) is done on the development set. Our evaluation metric is *Accuracy*: what proportion of tweets in each held-out test set are predicted correctly.

[5] Google once offered an online language-detection API, but this service is now deprecated; moreover, it was rate-limited and not licensed for research use (Lui and Baldwin, 2011).

[6] `https://github.com/saffsd/langid.py`

System	Arab.	Devan.	Cyrill.
Trained on Twitter Corpus:			
LogR: meta	79.8	74.7	82.0
LogR: chars	97.1	96.2	96.1
LogR: chars+meta	**97.4**	**96.9**	**98.3**
PPM	97.1	95.3	95.8
TextCat	96.3	89.1	90.3
Open-Domain: Trained on Other Materials:			
Google CLD	90.5	N/A	91.4
Lui and Baldwin '11	91.4	78.4	88.8
PPM (Wikip.)	**97.6**	95.8	95.7
PPM (All)	**97.6**	**97.1**	**95.8**
Trained on both Twitter and Other Materials:			
PPM (Wikip.+Twit)	**97.9**	97.0	95.9
PPM (All+Twit)	97.6	**97.9**	**96.0**

Table 4: LID accuracy (%) of different systems on held-out tweets. High LID accuracy on tweets is obtainable, whether training in or out-of-domain.

6 Results

For systems trained on the Twitter data, both our *LogR* and *PPM* system strongly outperform *TextCat*, showing the effectiveness of our implemented approaches (Table 4). Meta features improve *LogR* on each task. For systems trained on external data, *PPM* strongly outperforms other systems, making fewer than half the errors on each task. We also trained *PPM* on both the relatively small number of Twitter training samples and the much larger number of other materials. The combined system is as good or better than the separate models on each task.

We get more insight into our systems by seeing how they perform as we vary the amount of training data. Figure 1 shows that with only a few hundred annotated tweets, the *LogR* system gets over 90% accuracy, while performance seems to plateau shortly afterwards. A similar story holds as we vary the amount of out-of-domain training data for the *PPM* system; performance improves fairly linearly as exponentially more training data is used, but eventually begins to level off. Not only is *PPM* an effective system, it can leverage a lot of training ma-

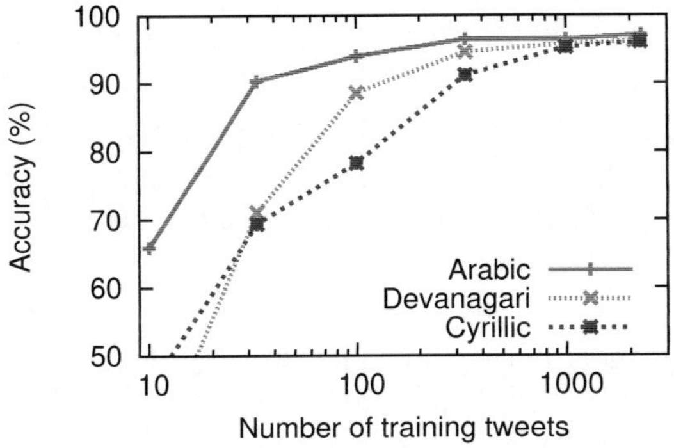

Figure 1: The more training data the better, but accuracy levels off: learning curve for *LogR*-chars (note log-scale).

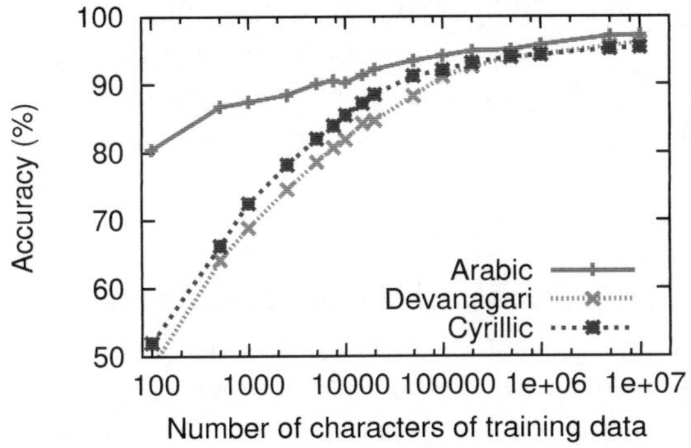

Figure 2: Accuracy of *PPM* classifier using varying amounts of Wikipedia training text (also on log-scale).

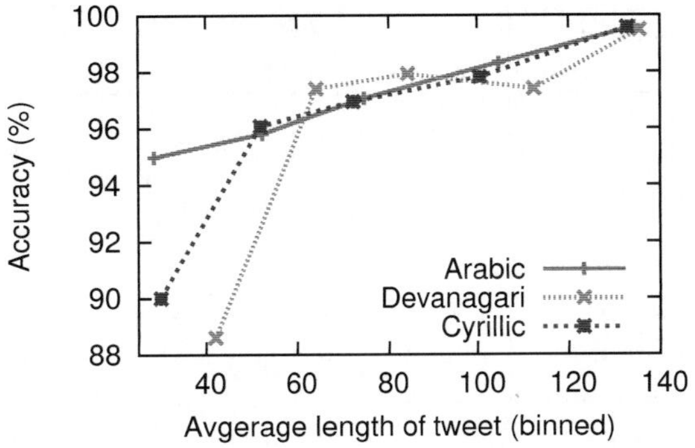

Figure 3: The longer the tweet, the better: mean accuracy of *LogR* by average length of tweet, with tweets grouped into five bins by length in characters.

Number of Tweets	1	2	3	4
Accuracy	97.0	98.7	98.8	98.9

Table 5: The benefits of aggregating predictions by user: Mean accuracy of *LogR*-chars as you make predictions on multiple Devanagari tweets at a time

terials in order to obtain its high accuracy.

In Figure 3, we show how the accuracy of our systems varies over tweets grouped into bins by their length. Performance on short tweets is much worse than those closer to 140 characters in length.

We also examined aggregating predictions over multiple tweets by the same user. We extracted all users with ≥4 tweets in the Devanagari test set (87 users in total). We then averaged the predictions of the *LogR* system on random subsets of a user's test tweets, making a single decision for all tweets in a subset. We report the mean accuracy of running this approach 100 times with random subsets of 1, 2, 3, and all 4 tweets used in the prediction. Even with only 2 tweets per user, aggregating predictions can reduce relative error by almost 60% (Table 5).

Encouraged by the accuracy of our systems on annotated data, we used our *PPM* system to analyze a large number of un-annotated tweets. We trained *PPM* models for 128 languages using data that includes Wikipedia (February 2012), news (e.g., BBC News, Voice of America), and standard corpora such as Europarl, JRC-Acquis, and various LDC releases. We then made predictions in the TREC Tweets2011 Corpus.[7]

We observed 65 languages in roughly 10 million tweets. We calculated two other proportions using auxiliary data:[8] (1) the proportion of *Wikipedia articles* written in each language, and (2) the proportion of *speakers* that speak each language. We use these proportions to measure a language's relative representation on Twitter: we divide the tweet-proportion by the Wikipedia and speaker proportions. Table 6 shows some of the most over-represented Twitter languages compared to Wikipedia. E.g., Indonesian is predicted to be 9.9 times more relatively common on Twitter than Wikipedia. Note these are predictions only; some English tweets may be falsely marked as other languages due to English impurities in our training sources. Nevertheless, the good representation of languages with otherwise scarce electronic resources shows the potential of using Twitter to build language-specific social media collections.

[7] `http://trec.nist.gov/data/tweets/` This corpus, developed for the TREC Microblog track (Soboroff et al., 2012), contains a two-week Twitter sample from early 2011. We processed all tweets that were obtained with a "200" response code using the *twitter-corpus-tools* package.

[8] From `http://meta.wikimedia.org/wiki/List_of_Wikipedias_by_speakers_per_article`

Language	Num. Tweets	% of Tot.	Tweets/ Wikip.	Tweets/ Speakers
Indonesian	1055	9.0	9.9	3.1
Thai	238	2.0	5.7	1.9
Japanese	2295	19.6	5.0	8.8
Korean	446	3.8	4.0	3.2
Swahili	46	0.4	3.4	0.4
Portuguese	1331	11.4	3.2	2.8
Marathi	58	0.5	2.9	0.4
Malayalam	30	0.3	2.2	0.4
Nepali	23	0.2	2.1	0.8
Macedonian	61	0.5	1.9	13.9
Bengali	25	0.2	1.9	0.1
Turkish	174	1.5	1.7	1.1
Arabic	162	1.4	1.6	0.3
Chinese	346	3.0	1.4	0.2
Spanish	696	5.9	1.4	0.7
Telugu	39	0.3	1.4	0.3
Croatian	79	0.7	1.3	6.1
English	2616	22.3	1.2	2.1

Table 6: Number of tweets (1000s) and % of total for languages that appear to be over-represented on Twitter (vs. proportion of Wikipedia and proportion of all speakers).

7 Related Work

Researchers have tackled language identification using statistical approaches since the early 1990s. Cavnar and Trenkle (1994) framed LID as a text categorization problem and made their influential TextCat tool publicly-available. The related problem of identifying the language used in speech signals has also been well-studied; for speaker LID, both phonetic and sequential information may be helpful (Berkling et al., 1994; Zissman, 1996). Insights from LID have also been applied to related problems such as dialect determination (Zaidan and Callison-Burch, 2011a) and identifying the native language of non-native speakers (Koppel et al., 2005).

Recently, LID has received renewed interest as a mechanism to help extract language-specific corpora from the growing body of linguistic materials on the web (Xia et al., 2009; Baldwin and Lui, 2010). Work along these lines has found LID to be far from a solved problem (Hughes et al., 2006; Baldwin and Lui, 2010; Lui and Baldwin, 2011); the web in general has exactly the uneven mix of style, languages, and lengths-of-text that make the real problem quite difficult. New application areas have also arisen, each with their own unique challenges, such as LID for search engine queries (Gottron and Lipka, 2010), or person names (Bhargava and Kondrak, 2010).

The multilinguality of Twitter has led to the development of ways to ensure language purity. Ritter et al. (2010) use "a simple function-word-driven filter. . . to remove non-English [Twitter] conversations," but it's unclear how much non-English survives the filtering and how much English is lost. Tromp and Pechenizkiy (2011) and Carter et al. (2013) perform Twitter LID, but only targeting six common European languages. We focus on low-resource languages, where training data is scarce. Our data and systems could enable better LID for services like `indigenoustweets.com`, which aims to "strengthen minority languages through social media."

8 Conclusions

Language identification is a key technology for extracting authentic, language-specific user-generated text from social media. We addressed a previously unexplored issue: LID performance on Twitter text in low-resource languages. We have created and made available a large corpus of human-annotated tweets in nine languages and three non-Latin writing systems, and presented two systems that can predict tweet language with very high accuracy.[9] While challenging, LID on Twitter is perhaps not as difficult as first thought (Carter et al., 2013), although performance depends on the amount of training data, the length of the tweet, and whether we aggregate information across multiple tweets by the same user. Our next step will be to develop a similar approach to handle *romanized* text. We also plan to develop tools for identifying *code-switching* (switching languages) within a tweet.

Acknowledgments

We thank Chris Callison-Burch for his help with the crowdsourcing. The first author was supported by the Natural Sciences and Engineering Research Council of Canada. The third author was supported by the BOLT program of the Defense Advanced Research Projects Agency, Contract No. HR0011-12-C-0015

[9]The annotated corpus and *PPM* system are available online at: `http://apl.jhu.edu/~paulmac/lid.html`

References

Timothy Baldwin and Marco Lui. 2010. Language identification: The long and the short of the matter. In *Proc. HLT-NAACL*, pages 229–237.

Dario Benedetto, Emanuele Caglioti, and Vittorio Loreto. 2002. Language trees and zipping. *Physical Review Letters*, 88(4):2–5.

Kay Berkling, Takayuki Arai, and Etienne Barnard. 1994. Analysis of phoneme-based features for language identification. In *Proc. ICASSP*, pages 289–292.

Aditya Bhargava and Grzegorz Kondrak. 2010. Language identification of names with SVMs. In *Proc. HLT-NAACL*, pages 693–696.

Andrej Bratko, Gordon V. Cormack, Bogdan Filipic, Thomas R. Lynam, and Blaz Zupan. 2006. Spam filtering using statistical data compression models. *JMLR*, 6:2673–2698.

John D. Burger, John Henderson, George Kim, and Guido Zarrella. 2011. Discriminating gender on Twitter. In *Proc. EMNLP*, pages 1301–1309.

Chris Callison-Burch and Mark Dredze. 2010. Creating speech and language data with amazon's mechanical turk. In *Proc. NAACL HLT 2010 Workshop on Creating Speech and Language Data with Amazon's Mechanical Turk*, pages 1–12.

Simon Carter, Wouter Weerkamp, and Manos Tsagkias. 2013. Microblog Language Identification: Overcoming the Limitations of Short, Unedited and Idiomatic Text. *Language Resources and Evaluation Journal*. (forthcoming).

William B. Cavnar and John M. Trenkle. 1994. N-gram-based text categorization. In *Proc. Symposium on Document Analysis and Information Retrieval*, pages 161–175.

John G. Cleary, Ian, and Ian H. Witten. 1984. Data compression using adaptive coding and partial string matching. *IEEE Transactions on Communications*, 32:396–402.

Jacob Eisenstein, Noah A. Smith, and Eric P. Xing. 2011. Discovering sociolinguistic associations with structured sparsity. In *Proc. ACL*, pages 1365–1374.

Rong-En Fan, Kai-Wei Chang, Cho-Jui Hsieh, Xiang-Rui Wang, and Chih-Jen Lin. 2008. LIBLINEAR: A library for large linear classification. *JMLR*, 9:1871–1874.

Clayton Fink, Jonathon Kopecky, Nathan Bos, and Max Thomas. 2012. Mapping the Twitterverse in the developing world: An analysis of social media use in Nigeria. In *Proc. International Conference on Social Computing, Behavioral Modeling, and Prediction*, pages 164–171.

Eibe Frank, Chang Chui, and Ian H. Witten. 2000. Text categorization using compression models. In *Proc. DCC-00, IEEE Data Compression Conference, Snowbird, US*, pages 200–209. IEEE Computer Society Press.

Rayid Ghani, Rosie Jones, and Dunja Mladenic. 2001. Automatic web search query generation to create minority language corpora. In *Proceedings of the 24th annual international ACM SIGIR conference on Research and development in information retrieval*, SIGIR '01, pages 432–433, New York, NY, USA. ACM.

Thomas Gottron and Nedim Lipka. 2010. A comparison of language identification approaches on short, query-style texts. In *Proc. ECIR*, pages 611–614.

Baden Hughes, Timothy Baldwin, Steven Bird, Jeremy Nicholson, and Andrew Mackinlay. 2006. Reconsidering language identification for written language resources. In *Proc. LREC*, pages 485–488.

Ann Irvine and Alexandre Klementiev. 2010. Using Mechanical Turk to annotate lexicons for less commonly used languages. In *Proc. NAACL HLT 2010 Workshop on Creating Speech and Language Data with Amazon's Mechanical Turk*, pages 108–113.

Emre Kiciman. 2010. Language differences and metadata features on Twitter. In *Proc. SIGIR 2010 Web N-gram Workshop*, pages 47–51.

Moshe Koppel, Jonathan Schler, and Kfir Zigdon. 2005. Determining an author's native language by mining a text for errors. In *Proc. KDD*, pages 624–628.

Marco Lui and Timothy Baldwin. 2011. Cross-domain feature selection for language identification. In *Proc. IJCNLP*, pages 553–561.

Paul McNamee. 2005. Language identification: a solved problem suitable for undergraduate instruction. *J. Comput. Sci. Coll.*, 20(3):94–101.

D. Pavelec, L. S. Oliveira, E. Justino, F. D. Nobre Neto, and L. V. Batista. 2009. Compression and stylometry for author identification. In *Proc. IJCNN*, pages 669–674, Piscataway, NJ, USA. IEEE Press.

Alan Ritter, Colin Cherry, and Bill Dolan. 2010. Unsupervised modeling of twitter conversations. In *Proc. HLT-NAACL*, pages 172–180.

Alan Ritter, Colin Cherry, and William B. Dolan. 2011. Data-driven response generation in social media. In *Proc. EMNLP*, pages 583–593.

Rion Snow, Brendan O'Connor, Daniel Jurafsky, and Andrew Y. Ng. 2008. Cheap and fast—but is it good?: evaluating non-expert annotations for natural language tasks. In *Proc. EMNLP*, pages 254–263.

Ian Soboroff, Dean McCullough, Jimmy Lin, Craig Macdonald, Iadh Ounis, and Richard McCreadie. 2012. Evaluating real-time search over tweets. In *Proc. ICWSM*.

William John Teahan. 2000. Text classification and segmentation using minimum cross-entropy. In *Proc. RIAO*, pages 943–961.

Erik Tromp and Mykola Pechenizkiy. 2011. Graph-based n-gram language identication on short texts. In *Proc. 20th Machine Learning conference of Belgium and The Netherlands*, pages 27–34.

Fei Xia, William Lewis, and Hoifung Poon. 2009. Language ID in the context of harvesting language data off the web. In *Proc. EACL*, pages 870–878.

Omar F. Zaidan and Chris Callison-Burch. 2011a. The arabic online commentary dataset: an annotated dataset of informal arabic with high dialectal content. In *Proc. ACL*, pages 37–41.

Omar F. Zaidan and Chris Callison-Burch. 2011b. Crowdsourcing translation: Professional quality from non-professionals. In *Proc. ACL*, pages 1220–1229.

Marc A. Zissman. 1996. Comparison of four approaches to automatic language identification of telephone speech. *IEEE Transactions on Speech and Audio Processing*, 4(1):31–44.

Processing Informal, Romanized Pakistani Text Messages

Ann Irvine and **Jonathan Weese** and **Chris Callison-Burch**
Center for Language and Speech Processing
Johns Hopkins University

Abstract

Regardless of language, the standard character set for text messages (SMS) and many other social media platforms is the Roman alphabet. There are romanization conventions for some character sets, but they are used inconsistently in informal text, such as SMS. In this work, we convert informal, romanized Urdu messages into the native Arabic script and normalize non-standard SMS language. Doing so prepares the messages for existing downstream processing tools, such as machine translation, which are typically trained on well-formed, native script text. Our model combines information at the word and character levels, allowing it to handle out-of-vocabulary items. Compared with a baseline deterministic approach, our system reduces both word and character error rate by over 50%.

1 Introduction

There are many reasons why systematically processing informal text, such as Twitter posts or text messages, could be useful. For example, during the January 2010 earthquake in Haiti, volunteers translated Creole text messages that survivors sent to English speaking relief workers. Machine translation (MT) could supplement or replace such crowdsourcing efforts in the future. However, working with SMS data presents several challenges. First, messages may have non-standard spellings and abbreviations ("text speak"), which we need to *normalize* into standard language. Second, many languages that are typically written in a non-Roman script use a romanized version for SMS, which we need to *deromanize*. Normalizing and deromanizing SMS messages would allow us to use existing MT engines, which are typically trained on well-formed sentences written in their native-script, in order to translate the messages.

With this work, we use and release a corpus of 1 million (4,195 annotated) anonymized text messages sent in Pakistan[1]. We deromanize and normalize messages written in Urdu, although the general approach is language-independent. Using Mechanical Turk (MTurk), we collect normalized Arabic script annotations of romanized messages in order to both train and evaluate a Hidden Markov Model that automates the conversion. Our model drastically outperforms our baseline deterministic approach and its performance is comparable to the agreement between annotators.

2 Related Work

There is a strong thread of research dedicated to normalizing Twitter and SMS informal English (Sproat et al., 2001). Choudhury et al. (2007) use a supervised English SMS dataset and build a character-level HMM to normalize individual tokens. Aw et al. (2006) model the same task using a statistical MT system, making the output context-sensitive at the cost of including a character-level analysis. More recently, Han and Baldwin (2011) use unsupervised methods to build a pipeline that identifies ill-formed English SMS word tokens and builds a dictionary of their most likely normalized forms. Beaufort et al. (2010) use a large amount of training data to supervise an FST-based French SMS normalizer. Li and Yarowsky (2008) present methods that take advantage of monolingual distributional similarities to identify the full form of abbreviated Chinese words. One challenge in working with SMS data is that public data is sparse (Chen and Kan, 2011). Transliteration is well-studied (Knight and Graehl, 1997; Haizhou et al., 2004; Li et al., 2010) and is usually viewed as a subproblem of MT.

With this work, we release a corpus of SMS messages and attempt to normalize Urdu SMS texts. Doing so involves the same challenges as normalizing English SMS texts and has the added complexity that we must also deromanize, a process similar to the transliteration task.

[1]See `http://www.cs.jhu.edu/~anni/papers/urduSMS/` for details about obtaining the corpus.

Original Message	**Vicky Kahan gaib ho tamam log? Lgta he parhai ho rhi he. Chalo shabash parh lo. MUBASHRA**
Language	Urdu
De-Romanization	کہاں غائب ہو تمام لوگ ، لگتا ہے پڑھائی ہو رہی ہے ، چلو شاباش پڑھ لو
English Translation	where are you people? seems everyone is studying. ok study its good

Figure 1: Example of SMS with MTurk annotations

3 Data and Annotation

Our Pakistani SMS dataset was provided by the Transnational Crisis Project, and it includes 1 million (724,999 unique) text messages that were sent in Pakistan just prior to the devastating July 2010 floods. The messages have been stripped of all metadata including sender, receiver, and timestamp. Messages are written in several languages, though most are in Urdu, English, or a combination of the two. Regardless of language, all messages are composed in the Roman alphabet. The dataset contains 348,701 word types, 49.5% of which are singletons.

We posted subsets of the SMS data to MTurk to perform language identification, followed by deromanization and normalization on Urdu messages. In the deromanization and normalization task, we asked MTurk workers to convert all romanized words into script Urdu and use full, non-abbreviated word forms. We applied standard techniques for eliminating noise in the annotation set (Callison-Burch and Dredze, 2010) and limited annotators to those in Pakistan. We also asked annotators to indicate if a message contained private, sensitive, or offensive material, and we removed such messages from our dataset.

We gathered deromanization and normalization MTurk annotations for 4,195 messages. In all experiments, we use 3,695 of our annotated SMS texts for training and 500 for testing. We found that 18% of word tokens and 44% of word types in the test data do not appear in the training data. An example of a fully annotated SMS is shown in Figure 1.

Figure 2 shows that, in general, productive MTurk annotators also tend to produce high quality annotations, as measured by an additional round of MTurk annotations which asked workers to choose the best annotation among the three we gathered. The raw average annotator agreements as measured by character and word level edit distance are 40.5 and 66.9, respectively. However, the average edit distances

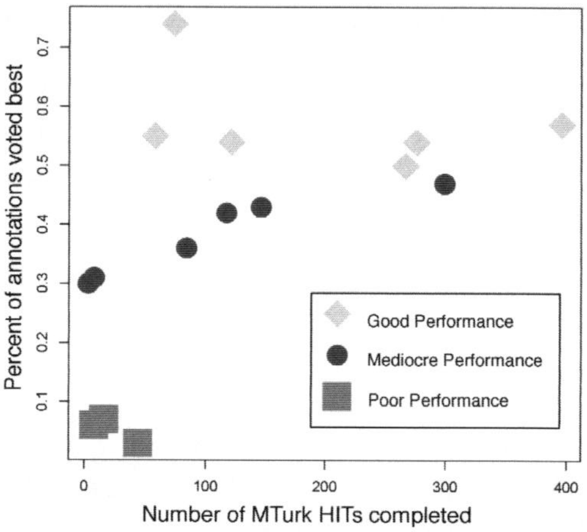

Figure 2: Productivity vs. percent of annotations voted best among three deromanizations gathered on MTurk.

Script	Romanizations [Frequency]	English
کرم	kram [3] karam [3] karm [2] karem [1]	grace
کونسا	konsa [6] kn sa [4] knsa [3] kon sa [2]	which
دوسروں	dusra [1] **2ro** [1] dosaro [1] dusron [1]	other people
خوش	khush [32] ki [1] khus [1]	happy
جگنو	jugno [1] ganjo [1]	firefly
باتیں	batein [7] baten [7] baatein [4] batain [4] btein [3]	chit-chat

Figure 3: Urdu words romanized in multiple ways. The Urdu word for "2" is pronounced approximately "du."

between 'good' MTurk workers (at least 50% of a worker's messages are voted best) and the deromanization which was voted best (when the two are different) are 25.1 (character) and 53.7 (word).

We used an automatic aligner to align the words in each Arabic script annotation to words in the original romanized message. The alignments show an average fertility of 1.04 script words per romanized word. Almost all alignments are one-to-one and monotonic. Since there is no reordering, the alignment is a simplified case of word alignment in MT.

Using the aligned dataset, we examine how Urdu words are romanized. The average entropy for non-singleton script word tokens is 1.49 bits. This means it is common for script words to be romanized in multiple ways (4.2 romanizations per script word on average). Figure 3 shows some examples.

4 Deromanization and Normalization

In order to deromanize and normalize Urdu SMS texts in a single step, we use a Hidden Markov Model (HMM), shown in Figure 4. To estimate the probability that one native-script word follows an-

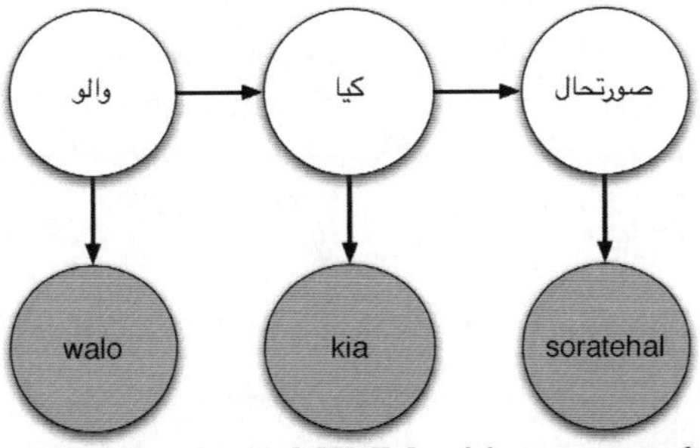

Figure 4: Illustration of HMM with an example from SMS data. English translation: "What's the situation?"

other, we use a bigram language model (LM) with add-1 smoothing (Lidstone, 1920) and compare two sources of LM training data.

We use two sources of data to estimate the probability of a romanized word given a script word: (1) a dictionary of candidates generated from automatically aligned training data, (2) a character-based transliteration model (Irvine et al., 2010).

If r is a romanized word and u is a script Urdu word, the dictionary-based distribution, $p_{\text{DICT}}(r|u)$, is given by relative frequency estimations over the aligned training data, and the transliteration-based distribution, $p_{\text{TRANS}}(r|u)$, is defined by the transliteration model scores. We define the model's emission probability distribution as the linear interpolation of these two distributions:

$$p_e(r|u) = (1-\alpha)p_{\text{DICT}}(r|u) + \alpha p_{\text{TRANS}}(r|u)$$

When $\alpha = 0$, the model uses only the dictionary, and when $\alpha = 1$ only the transliterations.

Intuitively, we want the dictionary-based model to memorize patterns like abbreviations in the training data and then let the transliterator take over when a romanized word is out-of-vocabulary (OOV).

5 Results and discussion

In the eight experiments summarized in Table 1, we vary the following: (1) whether we estimate HMM emissions from the dictionary, the transliterator, or both (i.e., we vary α), (2) language model training data, and (3) transliteration model training data.

Our baseline uses an Urdu-extension of the Buckwalter Arabic deterministic transliteration map. Even our worst-performing configuration outperforms this baseline by a large margin, and the best configuration has a performance comparable to the agreement among good MTurk workers.

	LM	Translit	α	CER	WER
1	News	—	Dict	41.5	63.3
2	SMS	—	Dict	38.2	57.1
3	SMS	Eng	Translit	33.4	76.2
4	SMS	SMS	Translit	33.3	74.1
5	News	SMS	Both	29.0	58.1
6	News	Eng	Both	28.4	57.2
7	SMS	SMS	Both	25.0	50.1
8	SMS	Eng	Both	**24.4**	**49.5**
Baseline: Buckwalter Determ.				64.6	99.9
Good MTurk Annotator Agreement				25.1	53.7

Table 1: Deromanization and normalization results on 500 SMS test set. Evaluation is by character (CER) and word error rate (WER); lower scores are better. "LM" indicates the data used to estimate the language model probabilities: News refers to Urdu news corpus and SMS to deromanized side of our SMS training data. "Translit" column refers to the training data that was used to train the transliterator: SMS; SMS training data; Eng; English-Urdu transliterations. α refers to the data used to estimate emissions: transliterations, dictionary entries, or both.

Unsurprisingly, using the dictionary only (Experiments 1-2) performs better than using transliterations only (Experiments 3-4) in terms of word error rate, and the opposite is true in terms of character error rate. Using *both* the dictionary derived from the SMS training data and the transliterator (Experiments 5–8) outperforms using only one or the other (1–4). This confirms our intuition that using transliteration to account for OOVs in combination with word-level learning from the training data is a good strategy[2].

We compare results using two language model training corpora: (1) the Urdu script side of our SMS MTurk data, and (2) the Urdu side of an Urdu-English parallel corpus,[3] which contains news-domain text. We see that using the SMS MTurk data (7–8) outperforms the news text (5–6). This is due to the fact that the news text is out of domain with respect to the content of SMS texts. In future work, we plan to mine Urdu script blog and chat data, which may be closer in domain to the SMS texts, providing better language modeling probabilities.

[2]We experimented with different α values on held out data and found its value did not impact system performance significantly unless it was set to 0 or 1, ignoring the transliterations or dictionary. We set $\alpha = 0.5$ for the rest of the experiments.

[3]LDC2006E110

Training Freq. bins			Length Diff. bins		
Bin	CER	WER	Bin	CER	WER
100+	9.8	14.8	0	23.5	43.3
10–99	15.2	22.1	1, 2	29.1	48.7
1–9	27.5	37.2	-1, -2	42.3	70.1
0	73.5	96.6	$\geq$3	100.3	100.0
			$\leq$-3	66.4	87.3

Table 2: Results on *tokens* in the test set, binned by training frequency or difference in character length with their reference. Length differences are number of characters in romanized token minus the number of characters in its deromanization. $\alpha = 0.5$ for all.

We compare using a transliterator trained on romanized/deromanized word pairs extracted from the SMS text training data with a transliterator trained on *English* words paired with their Urdu transliterations and find that performance is nearly equivalent. The former dataset is noisy, small, and in-domain while the latter is clean, large, and out-of-domain. We expect that the SMS word pairs based transliterator would outperform the English-Urdu trained transliterator given more, cleaner data.

To understand in more detail when our system does well and when it does not, we performed additional experiments on the token level. That is, instead of deromanizing and normalizing entire SMS messages, we take a close look at the kinds of romanized word tokens that the system gets right and wrong. We bin test set word tokens by their frequencies in the training data and by the difference between their length (in characters) and the length of their reference deromanization. Results are given in Table 2. Not surprisingly, the system performs better on tokens that it has seen many times in the training data than on tokens it has never seen. It does not perform perfectly on high frequency items because the entropy of many romanized word types is high. The system also performs best on romanized word types that have a similar length to their deromanized forms. This suggests that the system is more successful at the deromanization task than the normalization task, where lengths are more likely to vary substantially due to SMS abbreviations.

6 Summary

We have defined a new task: deromanizing and normalizing SMS messages written in non-native Roman script. We have introduced a unique new annotated dataset that allows exploration of informal text for a low resource language.

References

AiTi Aw, Min Zhang, Juan Xiao, and Jian Su. 2006. A phrase-based statistical model for SMS text normalization. In *Proceedings of COLING/ACL.*

Richard Beaufort, Sophie Roekhaut, Louise-Amélie Cougnon, and Cédrick Fairon. 2010. A hybrid rule/model-based finite-state framework for normalizing SMS messages. In *Proceedings of ACL.*

Chris Callison-Burch and Mark Dredze. 2010. Creating speech and language data with Amazon's Mechanical Turk. In *NAACL-NLT Workshop on Creating Speech and Language Data With Mechanical Turk.*

Tao Chen and Min-Yen Kan. 2011. Creating a live, public short message service corpus: The NUS SMS corpus. *Computation and Language*, abs/1112.2468.

Monojit Choudhury, Vijit Jain Rahul Saraf, Animesh Mukherjee, Sudeshna Sarkar, and Anupam Basu. 2007. Investigation and modeling of the structure of texting language. In *International Journal on Document Analysis and Recognition.*

Li Haizhou, Zhang Min, and Su Jian. 2004. A joint source-channel model for machine transliteration. In *Proceedings of ACL.*

Bo Han and Timothy Baldwin. 2011. Lexical normalisation of short text messages: Makn sens a #twitter. In *Proceedings of ACL.*

Ann Irvine, Chris Callison-Burch, and Alexandre Klementiev. 2010. Transliterating from all languages. In *Proceedings of the Association for Machine Translation in the America*, AMTA '10.

Kevin Knight and Jonathan Graehl. 1997. Machine transliteration. In *Proceedings of ACL.*

Zhifei Li and David Yarowsky. 2008. Unsupervised translation induction for Chinese abbreviations using monolingual corpora. In *Proceedings of ACL/HLT.*

Haizhou Li, A Kumaran, Min Zhang, and Vladimir Pervouchine. 2010. Report of NEWS 2010 transliteration generation shared task. In *Proceedings of the ACL Named Entities WorkShop.*

George James Lidstone. 1920. Note on the general case of the Bayes-Laplace formula for inductive or a posteriori probabilities. *Transactions of the Faculty of Actuaries*, 8:182–192.

Richard Sproat, Alan W. Black, Stanley F. Chen, Shankar Kumar, Mari Ostendorf, and Christopher Richards. 2001. Normalization of non-standard words. *Computer Speech & Language*, pages 287–333.

Author Index